Athenian Myths and Institutions

Athenian Myths and Institutions

Words in Action

WM. BLAKE TYRRELL

FRIEDA S. BROWN

New York   Oxford
OXFORD UNIVERSITY PRESS
1991

Oxford University Press

Oxford   New York   Toronto
Delhi   Bombay   Calcutta   Madras   Karachi
Petaling Jaya   Singapore   Hong Kong   Tokyo
Nairobi   Dar es Salaam   Cape Town
Melbourne   Auckland

and associated companies in
Berlin   Ibadan

Library of Congress Cataloging-in-Publication Data
Tyrrell, William Blake.
Athenian myths and institutions : words in action
Wm. Blake Tyrrell and Frieda S. Brown.
p. cm.   Includes bibliographical references and index.
1. Mythology, Greek.
2. Athens (Greece)—Religion.
3. Athens (Greece)—Civilization.
I. Brown, Frieda S. II. Title.
BL793.A76T97   1991
292.1'3—dc20   90-43853

ISBN 0-19-506718-5
ISBN 0-19-506719-3 (pbk.)

9 8 7 6 5 4 3 2 1

Printed in the United States of America
on acid-free paper

Preface

The perspectives developed in this book derive from myths as verbal constructs that are informed by the values, practices, and institutions of Athenian culture. We hope to show the ways in which myths both exemplify the categories of thought that describe the Athenian universe and condition their audience to those categories. We examine how mythmakers reflect, define, and defend the status quo, and we consider myths' bearing on ritual, the code of the warrior, marriage, and politics.

It has been our intention throughout this study to address a wider readership than that of professional classicists alone. To that end, we have glossed certain Greek terms. We believe that this book considers questions and provides directions for critical thinking that will be of value to university students of Classics as well as to a broader audience interested in Greek myths and mythmaking who would find useful a study that contextualizes Athenian mythmaking through a diversity of critical approaches. If we have failed to strike the proper balance, we trust we have erred in the direction of scholarship.

Our methodology combines traditional historical and literary criticism with the more modern approaches of anthropologists, feminist critics, and, in particular, the cultural historians Jean-Pierre Vernant, Marcel Detienne, and Pierre Vidal-Naquet. By grounding the myths in the customs, practices, and institutions of Greek society, these scholars have shown that myths are a verbal expression of beliefs, concepts, and practices operating in all aspects of culture.

Chapter 1 introduces the problems of defining myths and concludes that, for our purposes, a Greek myth is a tale rooted in Greek culture that recounts a sequence of events chosen by the maker of the tale to accommodate his own medium and objectives and to achieve particular effects in his audience.

Although the myths discussed in this study were active specifically in Athenian culture, we have treated the *Theogony* of the Boeotian poet Hesiod in Chapter 2 because Hesiod typifies Greek culture in imaging the cosmos from the male perspective.

Chapter 3 examines how myths validate and criticize what Arthur W.H. Adkins has called the *"aretē* standard." We evaluate Nestor's lesson in manly virtues in *Iliad* 11 as a prelude to Sophocles' treatment of the myth of Ajax, which illustrates the destructiveness of excessive adherence to that standard.

Chapter 4 studies the ways in which mythmakers explored the irresolvable flaw in Olympian blood sacrifice, namely, its resemblance to murder. The rituals of blood sacrifice and the Bouphonia provide the social context for interpreting Sophocles' *Ajax*.

Patriarchal mythmaking on marriage is the subject of Chapter 5. We begin by analyzing a particular form of marriage practiced commonly in Athens of the classical period and the dynamics which it reifies for Athenian mythmaking. Among the works we treat in this context are the *Homeric Hymn to Demeter*, Sophocles' *The Women of Trachis*, and Euripides' *Medea*. We also examine a secondary myth which conceals Aeschylus' maiming of the female in *Eumenides* beneath a supplement of juridical progress.

Chapters 6, 7, and 8 deal with different aspects of political life in Athens. In this sphere, mythic discourse provides a medium through which a group of people identify themselves as related to one another and distinct from similar groups by telling the same myths and, more importantly, by how they tell them to those within and without the group. Politicians and other mythmakers appropriated myths, exploiting for propagandistic purposes such myths as those of Theseus and Ion. We analyze the mythmaking displayed on the marbles of the Parthenon and in funeral orations over the dead, and end our discussion with a new reading of Sophocles' *Antigone*, relating it specifically to contemporary funeral oratory.

Unless otherwise indicated, translations from the Greek are ours, and all dates are B.C. Dates are given the first time a work, event, or author is named. For familiar names, we have retained the latinized spellings; for others, we have approximated the Greek orthography. The only footnotes are those that seemed to us necessary for a better understanding of the text. References within brackets in the text are to works listed in the bibliography.

Some of the material contained within these pages appeared earlier in different form in Wm. Blake Tyrrell's *Amazons: A Study in Athenian Mythmaking* and in his "The Unity of Sophocles' *Ajax*." We thank The Johns Hopkins University Press and the editor of *Arethusa*, respectively, for permission to use these texts here.

We express our thanks to Larry J. Bennett, whose separate work with Wm. Blake Tyrrell, "Sophocles' *Antigone* and Funeral Oratory," is forthcoming in *American Journal of Philology*.

East Lansing, Mich.   W.B.T.
June 1990   F.S.B.

Contents

Athenian Myths and Institutions

One

Introduction: Myths as Words in Action

Most of us formed our first impressions of Greek myths as children from the summaries and illustrated handbooks, movies, and cartoons that simplified and sanitized the doings of the gods and heroes. The stories were fun, and they impressed us as something uncomplicated, or frivolous. How, after all, could anyone take seriously such fantasy as Zeus's turning himself into a bull or Kronos' swallowing his children? In time, youthful skepticism was reinforced by the common opinion that myths are false and misleading. Commercial advertisements and political speeches abound with claims of exploding the "myth" of this or that by telling the truth. In the way of language, the word has become confused with the thing, and the meaningful place of Greek myths in the society that created them has become distorted, if not lost, through our own culture's estimation of myths.

The cartoonist Charles M. Schulz has captured the equivocation surrounding myths for Americans with Linus's myth of the Great Pumpkin. Linus is waiting at the pumpkin patch for the advent of the Great Pumpkin. Lucy, ever the pragmatist, chides him: "Santa Claus has elves to help him. What does the Great Pumpkin have, oranges?" Linus explains his creed ("This is what I believe") to Sally who thinks him mad. His is a tale of rewards for the faithful—toys for children the world over. The Great

Pumpkin never comes, and Linus blurts out his frustra-
tions: "Show up, Stupid!!!"—only to cover his blasphe-
mous mouth in horror. Next morning, Lucy tries to
browbeat him into cursing the Great Pumpkin and setting
himself free, but he cries: "Just wait 'til next year!!"

On another occasion, Linus reproves Sally by claiming
that Peppermint Patty also believes. "She's not like YOU.
She doesn't call 'the Great Pumpkin' a myth and a legend."
"How about a lie and a fraud?" retorts Sally. The exchange
shows that both share the common outlook that myths are
false and deceitful. They differ in that Linus's tale of the
Great Pumpkin, by being *true for him,* is not a myth but a
revealed word about his divinity. It is accompanied by a
creed and by ritual actions—waiting in the pumpkin patch
on a fixed night each year. Like many religious myths, his
tale organizes his life, promises future benefits, and alle-
viates his loneliness in the present. Lucy, who may believe
in Santa Claus (*her* true story), wants to break his faith,
presumably freeing him to think for himself, but he remains in the embrace of the authority imposed by his
myth. Linus's problems arise when he wants mythic beliefs to stand the test of concrete reality. It is one thing to
believe in the Second Coming, quite another to state an
hour for its occurrence.

The Greek word *mythos* denoted "anything said by the
mouth" and thereby simply opposed the spoken word to
the physical deed. In Homer, *mythos* also means a story
or tale—without any implication of truth or falsity. And
Plato (c. 429–347), the first to employ the term *mythologia,*
meant by it only the telling of stories. As narratives, myths
consist of words that relate events and actions. The narrative begins with one situation, passes through a middle
in which the situation is elaborated upon or altered, then
ends in quite another situation. The myth of Daphne, for
example, tells how Daphne, daughter of the river god Pe-
neus, was pursued by Apollo; she fled his embrace, pray-

ing for aid, and was changed into a laurel tree. Those stories which we know today as Greek myths were a vital, working, and formative medium in Greek society. For that reason, the study of Greek mythmaking, no less than the study of Greek history or philosophy, provides insights into a civilization which has value for itself and for our own.

G.S. Kirk has accurately pointed out that "the nature of myths is still, in spite of millions of printed words devoted to it, a confused topic" [1974, p. 17]. Given their many manifestations and complexities, myths have been richly mined by anthropologists, historians, psychologists, and social as well as literary critics. The same point might well be made about the definition of myth, which has been variously confounded with legend, folklore, allegory, and sacred tales. Part of the difficulty arises from attempting to determine what distinguishes a myth from another kind of narrative, say, a novel or a short story. A more insidious impediment is posed by the mode of the inquiry itself: what, in a word, constitutes the *mythic* element of a narrative? The question is that of the Platonic Socrates, heard here, for example, cross-examining Euthyphro, self-confessed expert on piety:

> Teach me the look (*eidos*) of piety, so that by observing it and using it as a model, I could say that what resembles it in the things you do or someone else does is pious and what does not resemble it I could deny is pious (*Euthyphro* 6e).

Once set on this path, the inquiry is locked into pursuing one form, one shape or idea (Plato's *eidos*) of the mythic, something eternally the same and ever like itself. Once the mythic has been defined, a story to be a myth must fall within the strict limits of that definition. Moreover, the definition itself may engender a particular method of interpretation or analysis. Yet scholars generally agree that no single approach suffices to explain everything in and about myths. There is also the danger that defining and analyzing myths, since we must do so in words, may become mythmaking activities in themselves. The present authors are not likely to escape these pitfalls entirely, but to avoid being entrapped by too refined a definition, we have opted for our purposes to define a Greek myth as *a tale rooted in Greek culture that recounts a sequence of events chosen by the maker of the tale to accommodate his own medium and purpose and to achieve particular effects in his audience.* As narratives that both exemplify and shape that culture, myths are words in action.

"I write what I believe to be true, for the stories of the Greeks are many and, it seems to me, absurd" (fr. 1). So the geographer Hecataeus (sixth century) begins his *Genealogies,* a treatise on the generations of mythic figures. He expresses his intention to tell the true, correct versions of the myths he surveys, but, to judge from the surviving fragments of his work, he simply recounted absurd versions of his own, which he created by applying logical and rational criteria to his subjects. Accordingly, Cerberus, for example, was not the "dog of Hades," but a serpent from Taenarum in the southern Peloponnesus whose poison instantly killed anyone it bit (fr. 27). Despite himself, Hecataeus could not escape the grip of those myths. An incident related by Herodotus (died c. 430–425) in his narrative of Egypt suggests a reason for his failure. "When Hecataeus, the prose writer, was in Thebes, he engaged in genealogy, tracing his lineage back to a god in the sixteenth generation" (2.143). Hecataeus' family was prominent among the nobles in Ionian Miletus and no doubt founded its claim to recognition, in part, on its divine ancestor. Its scion could not deny the reality preserved in his familial tradition. Self-interest or unquestioned belief or some other motive compelled him to accept the fundamental historicity of the stories he had heard from boyhood about his family's god. Scholars like Hecataeus might have quibbled with details and tried to make the myths more realistic, but not even they could deny their validity outright.

The authority imparted by time and by the voice of Homer and countless other poets had conditioned the Greeks to believe that their myths held truths. For them, the continued existence of the myth itself was apparently enough to guarantee the validity of its events and characters. Arrian (second century A.D.), a historian of Alexander the Great, writing eight centuries after the myths came to be questioned, affirms this in a typical response. While denying that Amazons were alive in Alexander's day (356–326), Arrian refuses to discredit their existence altogether because of the testimony of "so many authorities" (*Anabasis* 7.13.4–5).

Myths work the illusion of recording reality. Even modern scholars, falling under their spell, go in search of Priam's Troy or Odysseus' Ithaca. Until it can be demonstrated that myths are tied to a sequence of actual events and deeds of living persons, they will lack the essential element of a historical narrative: referentiality to real happenings. The word "history" denotes what happened in the past, the analysis of the evidence of what happened, and the creation of a narrative describing what happened; respectively, history denotes real events, a branch of knowledge, and a literary activity. That Athenians and Persians fought on the plain of Marathon in 490, no one seriously denies. A historian—Herodotus first in this case—gathers, sifts, and evaluates evidence for the battle to reconstruct, as far as his research allows, what happened. He then creates a narrative of the battle, which his imagination, literary talent, and prejudices influence. Every fighter that day fought his own Marathon. Those Marathons, although real for the individuals involved, perished with them. The Marathon that exists is the Marathon of the historian's sources and craft; it is historical by virtue of its embodiment in a narrative written by a historian. If the evidence did not permit analysis or no historian chose to analyze what was available, Marathon, no less real, would not be a historical event.

Like history, myths embody events in narratives; however, they refer not to real events but to other narratives. Myths recall different versions of the same story as well as other myths. The idea of a son who marries his mother opens to the imagination the possibility of a son who kills his mother and vice versa. In this sense, Oedipus implies Orestes, and Orestes, Oedipus, as well as any number of permutations of over- and underevaluating kinship ties. Neither denotes a real person or a unique set of events. Since a given version of the myth of Orestes or Oedipus presupposes an earlier one, such questions as "Who told the story first?" and "In what form was it first told?" have aroused extensive discussion. The pursuit of an "original" which, in any case, belongs to an irrecoverable past, is a fruitless endeavor. It tacitly assumes that no one had ever told a story about a son killing his mother until one day someone had the idea and told it in a way that forever remained *the* version of which later ones are distortions and corruptions.

To the contrary, myths refer to relations inherent in the culture's value system and may be told with manifold emphases and variations within the confines of their basic plots. They constitute a discourse, a verbal medium, through which members of the community—those who share the same myths—use the past to talk about the present. They communicate with one another *through* but not *about* their past. Myths contain the same oppositions and structures that characterize other social institutions. They validate and sanction civilization as a human construct by relating it to and distinguishing it from the divine and the bestial. They depict in imaginary form a model to be emulated, as well as the destructive forces active in society, which, left unvented, could rupture the social bond. Myths provide examples of how things go when they go "right" and when they go "wrong." Heracles of Sophocles' *The Women of Trachis* not only illustrates how not to act in marriage; he incarnates the lust felt and feared by the Athenians. Society is not a static, once-erected-ever-stable entity, but a fragile arresting of centrifugal forces. Myths serve as one medium through which its members attempt to hold off total fragmentation.

Greek myths indirectly reproduce in narrative form the values and beliefs, prescriptions and regulations, customs and practices that simultaneously reflected and helped shape a warlike, imperialistic society of aristocrats. We may perhaps draw an analogy with the modern technology of computers. A myth corresponds to a program in that it provides the maker of the tale with an easily remembered sequence of events. The myth, like the program, allows access to a data bank through the technique of the maker's craft (his "hardware"). Since the data consist of things defining the identity of the group, the meanings derived from the data through their encoding in the tale depend upon the listener's understanding, attitude, and social position. The polyvalence of myths, their ability to convey meaning and appear significant to people of wide-ranging sorts, cultures, and historical periods, is the necessary result.

The mythic element of a story, then, does not reside in its plot or a particular "making." The power of the message, "Please come here," does not derive from the computer. (By contrast, "Mr. Watson, come here, I want you," is unique: it gains meaning from the instrument as the first intelligible words communicated by telephone.) A story is endowed with the mythic by the receptors, who, consciously or unconsciously, grant it its power to make them consider their value system, their conceptual universe, their world within and without. The extent to which the narrative fulfilled cultural needs and appealed to the concerns and interests of those telling and listening to it contributed to its survival, and that survival led over time to the designation of the Greek *mythos* as a myth. In other words, that a story is old or traditional is not its mythic element; that element must be assigned to the audience that kept the story alive. In a very real sense, successive generations of tellers and listeners from the Romans on, ourselves and our readers included, have continued to make Greek *mythoi* into myths.

Accordingly, the mythic has no fixed look or Platonic form. It functions within the dynamic between the culture as a system and senders and receivers of messages communicated in myths. Modern students of Homer's *Iliad* often find the repeated combat scenes tiresome and hardly relevant, whereas the poet's audiences among ancient Greeks at some time must have found them meaningful. Similarly, most Americans know the story of George Washington and the cherry tree. But how many perceive it as a tale of America's defiance of old Europe, the taming of a new frontier, the purposeful but innocent destruction of the old, and paternal approval of youthful rebellion? [Robertson, 1980, pp. 10–14]. We do not readily see these applications of the myth to American society, because America is no longer that of the teller Mason Weems and of McGuffey's *Readers*, the popularizing medium of his story.

By making the receptors the final arbiter of what is mythic, we recognize the essential role that psychological, sociological, political, and other motives play in communication between mythmakers and audiences. On the other hand, we cannot reproduce the feelings and thoughts of an ancient audience. We therefore must imagine an audience that has knowledge of Athenian social institutions, such as the warrior ethic and marriage, knowledge that we postulate from the available evidence. In studying the myths through this hypothetical audience, we seek to approach what Athenians found mythic in these stories and how these stories defended and defined Greek, specifically Athenian, culture against disorder and the forces of entropy.

Athenians, like all Greeks, defined their world as something apart from the divine above and the bestial below, apart from the female and from the foreign. No matter whether Thales (early sixth century) or Socrates (c. 469–399) voiced the following sigh of relief, it is typically Greek:

> [Thales or Socrates] kept saying that he gave thanks to Fortune for three reasons: "first, that I was born a human being and not a beast; secondly, that I was born a man and not a woman; third, that I was born a Greek and not a foreigner" (Diogenes Laertius, *Lives of Eminent Philosophers* 1.33).

Aristotle (384–322) in *Politics* expresses a similar conception of the world:

> If each individual when separate is not self-sufficient, he must be related to the whole *polis* (city-state) as other parts are to their whole. The man who is incapable of entering into a partnership or who is so self-sufficient that he has no need to do so, must be either a beast or a god (1253a).

The ideal was the adult Greek male. Such men inhabited a *polis* in partnership with other men, the whole having precedence over its parts. Any man who did not need partners because of his self-sufficiency belonged by definition outside the *polis* in the realms of the divine or the bestial. The methods and strategies of interpretation in this book are based upon that outlook.

Our methodology combines traditional historical and literary criticism with the more modern approaches of anthropologists, feminists, and, in particular, the cultural historians Jean-Pierre Vernant, Marcel Detienne, and Pierre Vidal-Naquet. By grounding the myths in the customs, practices, and institutions of Greek society, these scholars have shown that myths are a verbal expression of beliefs, concepts, and practices operating in all aspects of culture. What emerges is the view that myths reflect the categories of thought which structure the universe and, at the same time, acculturate their receptors to it. The Greeks conceived of the universe in polar terms, that is, they viewed and defined themselves as Greek, male, free, adult, and warlike as opposed to others who were *barbaroi* (foreign), female, slave, young or old, pacified. The pervasiveness of such polar thinking opens the Greek myths to an approach that concentrates on the oppositions that differentiate one group from another and on the circumstances under which those oppositions break down. Myths rarely deal with the normal because, in part, the norm is neither interesting nor exciting. A woman's place was in the home tending the children and watching over her husband's property. She could no more leave the house alone than take up the warrior's life. But the myth of the Amazon, a female warrior, derived from Greek culture when the values associated with the male/female opposition were lost by imagining the daughter's refusal to leave her mother for a husband chosen by her father. By telling what happens when those values are lost, myths teach what is culturally valued. Myths act to assert, in the face of entropic forces, the status quo.

Greek mythmaking is one of many media that conditioned the members of Greek society in the meaning and expectations of their culture. The major structures found in myths, immortal/mortal, human/bestial, and male/female, were not confined to myths but pervaded all of Greek life. They and countless others imposed order on the physical world and created the Greeks' conceptual universe.

Two

Hesiod's Myth of the Birth of the Cosmos

Human beings, we assume, have always told stories about the world they inhabit. It would appear we cannot live in "unspoken" space. Verbalizing the world, however, goes beyond naming its features. A name confers upon a body of water meanings that it does not have as a natural phenomenon. A word, a sound we recognize as denoting something, makes a body of water a "river" which, in turn, can take on other meanings. It can be an obstacle, a borderline, an avenue for commerce, a source of food, gold, or pleasure, the place where a drowning occurred. These identities incorporate it into "spoken" space and become so integral a part of our physical world that we tend to overlook the fact that they are constructs of human experience and imagination. In this way, we "create" the world around us.

Similarly, humans need to know how their world originated. In the myth under discussion in this chapter, a universe unfolds through successive generations of gods, a process culminating in the organization of the cosmos under Zeus. Primordial changes take place in much the same way that things change in Hesiod's world within the family: parents produce children, the daughter serves her father's interests by being given away in marriage, and the son replaces the father as the head of the household [Arthur, 1982]. Founding events are patterned on the model of human society and "descend," as it were, from the heavens of the primordial past to orient members of the community to the cosmos and to validate and justify their social order. Such myths are not the products of scientific curiosity but of the need for oneness within and without the known universe, the need to feel secure amid the chaos of a hostile world.

All peoples have cosmogonic myths. They may not be aware of them, since these myths blend in with "reality," but, whether consciously or not, they apprehend reality through a looking glass consisting of their myths. The first settlers in America disregarded the natives in order to tell the story of a land empty and desolate until it was discovered by Columbus [Robertson, 1980, pp. 33–37]. America became the New World, a garden of opportunity for new beginnings, a place of enrichment for those oppressed in the Old World, and a locus of progress and discovery based upon technology and faith in the Christian deity. Centuries later, the myth of the New World still defines for Americans the space around them as well as their national identity. They receive the message through advertising, among other media. Andy Rooney on *60 Minutes* [7/31/83] cited "new," "natural," "light," "save," "free," "rich," "real," "fresh," "extra," and "discover(y)" as the ten most common words in advertising. Powerfully charged, these words evoke the dreams and aspirations promised by our founding myth: "Discover," "fresh," "new," and "light" (that is, unburdened) evoke promise and opportunity; "natural" and "real," what the seeker may find here; "extra," "rich," and "save," what accrues from initiative. The message: Eden/America holds out material rewards obtainable without suffering the oppressions of the Old World. Advertisements try to induce us to buy things by evoking the founding myth of America, its myth of rebirth in a garden paradise.

Sometimes in reading Hesiod or, for that matter, the

myths of any people, we are struck by how silly and con-
trived they seem. The myth of Athena's birth from Zeus's
head strikes readers as particularly absurd, yet it plays a
crucial role in achieving order and stability in Hesiod's
universe. Equally absurd is the American myth of the New
World which we may regain through an elixir, be it tooth-
paste, a new car, clothes, or diet. Rather than how Greeks
could believe in such things, we do better to ask how they
could *not* believe in them. Too much was at stake for Hesiod and his contemporaries to dare otherwise.

What comes closest to the Greeks' cosmogonic myth was
composed by Hesiod in the late eighth century. His poetry
portrays him as a farmer who herded sheep on Mount
Helicon near Askra in Boeotia rather than as a professional
bard, and scholars have assumed that he learned the craft
of singing by listening to others. His *Theogony* belongs to
an oral poetry that probably reached back to the Mycenaean Age and was practiced across the Mediterranean as
far as India. Other poets surely preceded Hesiod, but it
was he who recorded his version or had it written down
so that it survived until the Classical Age to reach the
librarians of Alexandria and Pergamum. Writing gave Hesiod's work the permanence that allowed later generations
of Greeks to make him a founding source of their conception of the gods. In the sense that he has composed a
cosmogonic myth, Hesiod relates the birth (*-gony*) of the
universe (*cosm-*) and, more specifically in the *Theogony*, the
birth of the gods (*the-*). No mere storyteller, he imagines
and constructs the way in which the cosmos was born and
how it came to be ruled by Zeus, using the only information available to him, the stories about the gods that he
inherited.

Hesiod's cosmogony begins with the birth of Chaos or
Void. He is silent about the cosmos before the birth of
Chaos. Pronounced "khawos," the Greek word does not
denote a state of primal confusion but a gaping abyss lo-

cated between Gaia above and the underworld Tartarus below. This yawning gap, filled with darkness, gives birth to Erebus, god of the infernal regions, and to "black Night." Next are born Gaia (Earth), Tartarus, and Eros (Sexual Passion), not from Chaos but, Hesiod says, one after another. The reproductive force Eros, innate in the universe from its inception, cannot be resisted and subdues "the mind and thoughtful counsel of all gods and men" (122). Consequently, Eros operates as an irrepressible force for change in Hesiod's world through the begetting and bearing of children. With the continuous birth of children, usually from two parents but also from the mother alone, Hesiod incarnates and populates the universe. For him, all things—day and night, sea and mountains, gods and mortals—must be born, and that belief generates the many genealogies and long lists of names in his *Theogony*. His genealogies not only account for the origin of natural objects and deities but also demonstrate how Hesiod, the poet, preserves their memory by skillfully working them into the restrictions of his rhythmic pattern.

The primal parents, Chaos and Gaia, together encompass all that is and will be. As cosmogony develops by generations, figures become successively narrower in scope and more clearly defined in meaning. At the same time, the cosmos evolves from figures embodying aspects of nature—Earth, Sky, Sea, Mountains—to those representing elements of culture—Eunomia (Observance of Laws), Dike (Justice), Eirene (Peace)—and progresses from the primacy of the female to the dominance of the male. Hesiod brings about this evolution through the displacement of cosmic powers. Since birth is, in the beginning, the only manifestation of power, Ouranos initiates a struggle for dominance over his mother and sexual partner Gaia; in the next generations, Kronos and Zeus combine the sexual conflict with a political scheme to maintain kingship. This theme, called by scholars "Kingship in

Heaven," is basically that of a succession of three gods, each of whom seizes power from the one before him. The third and lasting ruler must overcome the challenge of a monster acting on behalf of the deposed second ruler. The myth, with numerous variations, was told not only in Hesiod's Greek but also by the Hurrians, Hittites, Babylonians, Assyrians, Phoenicians, and Iranians [Littleton, pp. 83–121].

Hesiod typifies his culture in imaging the cosmos from a male perspective. The female becomes Other, the outsider whose resources, sex, procreativity, and work are nonetheless essential for the creation and continuance of culture. In moving toward male rule under Zeus, Hesiod employs different strategies or narrative techniques in speaking about male and female figures. He consolidates male power by incorporating into the rule of Kronos and Zeus elements of the power of their predecessors. Each thus becomes stronger by having available to him the strengths of earlier dominant males. By contrast, Hesiod fragments the original wholeness and unity of Chaos and Gaia through the proliferation of female figures. Distributing powers and attributes among many females, he weakens female force and assimilates it into male rule [Arthur, 1982].

In the proem (1–115), Hesiod relates the birth of the Muses and their power and privileges among men. They are the daughters of Mnemosyne (Memory) and Zeus. Mnemosyne, a Titan god born of Gaia and Ouranos in the generation before Zeus and the Olympians, encompasses more than the ability to remember. She is memorization, the faculty that permits the bard to recall the formulas, rhythms, themes, and episodes comprising his craft. Mnemosyne enables him to be the repository of his culture's past, whether in the form of the deeds of gods and heroes or of precedents and customs. Zeus appropriates this power as his own by impregnating Mnemosyne with the nine Muses. He benefits by gaining the mother's prerogative, memorization, something whose worth Ouranos and Kronos failed to realize. Zeus makes use of her memorization through daughters who live with him on Olympus, forever unwed, and who sing not for their own pleasure and profit but for the delight of their father. Moreover, they sing, as the *Theogony* itself exemplifies, about Zeus's establishment of a moral and political order in the universe. Hesiod's ideal and stable relationship between the sexes is that between the father and his virgin daughters, who are dedicated to furthering his interests. A more striking and significant instance is that of Zeus and his daughter Athena, who is born motherless from her father's head. Through the faculty inherited from their mother, the Muses preserve the past accomplishments of their father. They fulfill Mnemosyne's potential; indeed, they are that potential, although each of the nine individually embodies but one part of it. What that potential is becomes clear when we examine what Hesiod says about them. Their father has kingship in heaven (71). They dance (4, 7) and send forth their beautiful (68), passionate (65) voices. They sing (66, 69), celebrating (67) the customs and manners of all and delighting (37, 51) their father. The black earth laughs as they sing their hymns (70). They live with the Graces and Desire among bounteous festivals (65). After first telling what the Muses are like and what they do, Hesiod—probably the first to do so—derives their names from those qualities and activities. Before him, they were likely known simply as "the Muses." They are now Cleio (Celebrator), Euterpe (Good Delight), Thaleia (Bounteous Festivity), Melpomene (Singing One), Terpsichore (Delight in Dance), Erato (Lovely One), Polymnia (Many Hymns), Ourania (Heavenly One), and Calliope (Beautiful Voice) (77–79).

In describing the Muses, Hesiod defines what he, the bard as their servant, does and what effects he has on his audience [Havelock, 1963, pp. 97–111; 145–60]. Moving rhythmically and accompanying himself on the lyre, the bard prompts his memory to hymn the gods and celebrate heroes. He elicits delight, pleasure, and even erotic passion in his listeners, who, we imagine, are already relaxed by the festivities at hand. In this way, the Muses accomplish "the forgetfulness of evils and the cessation of anxieties" (55). They do not exercise their powers directly, however, but through the agency of the poet. Like his Zeus, Hesiod takes their powers as his own and benefits from them.

Gaia at first represents that totality out of which the gods, including Zeus, descend. Having control over her own sexuality, she produces without the need for a male. With the birth of Ouranos, who becomes her mate and seeks control over her body, Gaia is diminished to all female. Ouranos, who hates his unborn children because they are fearful, prevents Gaia from giving birth to them, pushes them down into Gaia, and will not let them come into the light. In pain despite her vastness, Gaia devises a "deceitful evil trick" (160). She invents adamant, the hard metal of the gods (perhaps iron) and fashions a sickle. She explains its purpose to the children within her, who are at first struck with fear. Then, out of hatred for his "lusty" father, the youngest child, Kronos of crooked cunning, agrees to her plan. Gaia hides him in ambush (174) and together, mother and son defeat the father in a grim scene. While Ouranos, desiring Gaia, embraces her, Kronos reaches from his ambush and castrates him with the sickle. He avenges his father's "boldness" and achieves the birth of his siblings. Members of the same family, Ouranos and Kronos direct their hostilities at its very foundations, kinship ties. But the success of the deceitful and evil scheme has its price, and the children will pay for their father's blood.

We do well at this point to remember that Hesiod's actual audience *listened* to his poems, a fact whose implications often go unnoticed by a reading audience. To read Hesiod as an authorial audience, that is, one for whom he may have intended his text [Rabinowitz, p. 117], we must ignore the distinction created on the printed page between Gaia the divinity with upper case G and gaia as earth with lower case g or e. Through orthography or vocabulary, the translator or editor in accord with his own understanding of the text creates a distinction which Hesiod's listeners, hearing the same sound in its four grammatical forms over and over, would hardly perceive. Gaia and Ouranos are playing out a power struggle for mastery of her procreativity that ends in his castration. Blood from his genitals spatters Gaia. The drops fall onto the physical earth just as the genitals fall into the sea, but they also fall on Gaia the goddess. The translator necessarily compartmentalizes G/gaia's duality into two distinct entities. That problem plus the word's transparent referentiality to the earth and/ or the refusal to accept the defilement of the goddess have prevented critics from appreciating that this is happening to earth and divinity alike. The blood seeping into her crevices quickens her vastness and befouls her with a violent substitute for Ouranos' semen. For her deceit, Gaia is punished by being impregnated with the Erinyes who will exact vengeance for Ouranos from her other children.

Because Gaia and Ouranos are the primal parents, rivalry between trickery and strength to gain their due is now innate to the universe. Strength alone will not secure Zeus's position as king of the cosmos; he must overcome cunning. Moreover, the birth of Aphrodite from the foam-enclosed genitals of her father diminishes Gaia's fullness and disperses the power of Eros. The desire that drew Ouranos to Gaia henceforth attends his daughter Aphrodite. The effect is twofold. Gestated by the sea, Hesiod's Aphrodite has no mother, nor will she bear children. She offers gods and men the delights of sexual union without the necessity to submit to the process of change and to the forfeiture of male privileges that result from the birth of a new generation. Also, the charms of the female, now freed, cause trouble, since they operate outside the proper function of sexual union, the bearing of children.

Ouranos is less a king than a patriarch whose authority depends upon his fertility. He hates his children for being what they are, the fearful product of his own irresistible sex drive. Once deprived of the capacity to gratify his erotic desire, he recedes into the background. Although he joins Gaia in prophesying to Kronos and Zeus, the real force remains with Gaia.

Kronos is a king in heaven. He fears the birth of a son because of Gaia's prophecy that he will be overthrown by his son who will then assume the royal privilege. Besides monstrous and fearful progeny, female procreativity threatens the male with displacement. This dynamic of Hesiod's cosmogony reflects the tensions felt by the husband and father who sires a son not only as his heir and protector but also as his successor in the mastery over his household. Kronos attempts to avert his fate by swallowing each child as it is born. Like his father before him, he assaults the procreative process. However, he reverses his predecessor's effort by subjecting the children to his own stomach/womb (the Greek *nēdys* denotes both organs); that is, he tries to maintain his dominion by not merely obstructing but by nullifying the birth process. When Rhea is about to bear her youngest, she begs her parents, Gaia and Ouranos, for help in foiling Kronos' scheme. Gaia tells her to go to Crete, where Zeus is born. Gaia tends him and gives Kronos a stone wrapped in swaddling clothes, which he swallows. Later, Gaia again deceives Kronos, and he vomits up the stone, which is followed by Zeus's brothers and sisters. Zeus erects the stone as "a marvel and a portent to mortal men" (500), memorializing both the wonder of female cleverness and power and its ominous implications for males.

Having recorded Ouranos' failure, Hesiod gives Kronos the capacity to improve on his father's scheme by having him mate with a sister instead of the mother and by permitting birth to take place before hiding his children. Despite being outwitted by Gaia, Kronos clearly shows greater cunning than Ouranos. Rhea, on the other hand, is weakened. She does not act as a mother against her mate but must appeal as a daughter to her parents. She neither conceives nor executes Gaia's "shifty plan" and represents a further diminution of the female.

Hesiod relates the myth of Prometheus (535–616) out of the chronological sequence of his narrative. Zeus has already become king of the cosmos when he matches wits with Prometheus. His battle with Kronos and the Titans in which he won sovereignty has yet to be fought. Apparently disturbed by Kronos' fate, Hesiod leaps ahead to demonstrate Zeus's superiority over cunning. He leaves no doubt that this is his intention as he states the moral of the episode: "Thus it is not possible to beguile or outstrip the intelligence and purpose of Zeus" (613), for even crafty Prometheus failed. It is Prometheus that Zeus gets the better of by his intelligence, but Hesiod's language betrays a deeper concern with Gaia and trickery itself.

Gaia conceives the ruse of the sickle and ambush, which Hesiod calls a "deceitful evil trick" (*doliē kakē technē*). Kronos is deceived (*dolōtheis*) into disgorging Zeus and the other Olympian gods. Variations of the phrase *doliē kakē technē* occur six times, five in the narrative of Prometheus' carving trick. Prometheus lays out the white bones "in a deceitful trick" (540) and, in addressing Zeus, does not forget his "deceitful trick" (547). Zeus recognizes the "deceit" (551); anger comes over his spirit when he sees the ox's white bones "in deceitful trick" (555). Zeus admits that Prometheus did not forget his "deceitful trick" (560) and gives men a "deceit" (589) of his own, Woman. In contrast with the Metis episode, in which Hesiod allows Zeus to usurp female trickery in seducing Metis, the Prometheus episode shows Zeus triumphant over trickery in a male rival, while it also opposes Zeus's "intelligence and purpose" to Gaia's "deceitful evil trick." Hesiod's language reveals that Prometheus stands for Gaia. Since Gaia's deceptiveness can no more be eradicated than Gaia herself, Hesiod, consciously or not, provides Zeus with victory by means of a surrogate. Unlike Gaia, Prometheus can be chained to a rock, immobile and helpless, his wily resourcefulness thwarted [Detienne and Vernant, pp. 57–92].

The episode begins abruptly: the gods, about to withdraw to Olympus, meet with men at Mekone to make a settlement. Hesiod tells neither what they are settling nor why it is Prometheus who cuts up the ox, but since in the course of events men receive fire, a gift usually attributed to Prometheus, it is not surprising that Hesiod has him also do the carving trick. He needs no reason for Prometheus' trickery; the latter is by nature a trickster, motivated by his own caprice and not yet the champion of mankind of Aeschylus' *Prometheus Bound.* Hesiod calls him "good Prometheus" (565) for stealing the fire, but, in the long run, men are much worse off for his one-upmanship with Zeus.

> Prometheus concealed the flesh and innards rich with fat in the ox's stomach and, putting the stomach into the hide, placed it before Zeus. Before men he placed the white bones of the ox arranged attractively in a deceitful trick and concealed in gleaming fat (538–541).

Because Hesiod intends to show the superiority of Zeus's intelligence and purpose over Prometheus' cunning, his

Zeus sees through the elaborate scheme. In other accounts of the trick, Zeus is not so provident. With no small measure of irony, Hyginus (second century A.D.), in his manual on astronomy, grants that Zeus is duped: "Zeus did not act with the brains of a god, nor did he foresee everything, as befits a god; but since I have decided to believe in stories, Zeus, deceived by Prometheus...chose the bones for his half" (2.15). Hesiod's Zeus lets himself be tricked because he is planning "evils," *kaka* in Greek, for men (551). Evils surely include being deprived of the divine presence, so that the events at Mekone where the gods are withdrawing to Olympus, no longer to dine on earth with men, take on added significance. We cannot assume Zeus foresees the theft of fire, but Hesiod sees it all, all the evils that mark the human condition—woman, marriage, work, and death. Hesiod is telling the story, using Zeus and Prometheus to explain what already exists in his world. The knowledge that the *kaka* of his own life came from Zeus had to produce tension in one whose lord god was Zeus.

Zeus chooses the portion that is attractive on the outside but contains inedible bones on the inside, establishing forever the division of the victim in sacrifice [Vernant, 1980, pp. 168–85]. Men receive the meat; then the bones and thigh pieces are wrapped in fat and burned on the altar with incense and sent to the gods in the smoke. More than providing a reason for the divisions in sacrifice, the myth explains sacrifice as one means of defining civilization by establishing a hierarchy: animals are sacrificed and eaten, men sacrifice and eat cooked meat, and gods receive sacrifice and eat no meat. Men are thereby elevated above the animals, but they remain forever below the gods, since they must sacrifice and eat meat to survive. Every sacrifice betokens civilization as something distinct from the divine above and the bestial below.

Once men have obtained meat, they are assured of survival, since a benefit conferred in Hesiod's universe cannot be taken back. But the good that is meat can be counter-balanced by an evil. Zeus removes fire from the trees, where it had been available to men by the chance occur-rence of lightning and friction of branches. The notion, as M.L. West [pp. 323–24] contends, is that fire is a substance that can be rubbed out of the trees. Without fire, men, unable to cook their food, would starve, for unlike the animals, men do not eat meat raw. Sacrifice, then, imposes another limitation upon the men at Mekone as well as another definition of civilization: to be civilized is to eat cooked, not raw meat.

Prometheus responds to Zeus's removal of fire with an-other trick. He hides Zeus's heavenly fire in the pithy center of a fennel stalk where it smolders unseen. Like many cultures, the Greeks located the source of fire in the heavens and attributed its presence on earth to a theft. After the gift of fire, men no longer depend upon chance for the cooking fire; now, they control fire. But theirs is very different from the fire of Zeus. His springs by his own will from the thunderbolt, while men's fire demands fuel acquired by work, for without fuel, it quickly dies.

Prometheus' cunning is a shiftiness that appeared to the Greeks as motion, so he is tied down. Zeus, angered by Prometheus' trickery, binds him in chains and drives a pillar through them, rooting him fast. Zeus is also angered because, with the control of fire, men move closer to the gods, as it were, *up* to them: "It stung high-thundering Zeus anew and angered him in his heart when he saw the far-seen beam of fire among men" (567–69). Zeus pushes them *down* by bestowing upon them Woman, a thing made of earth, the very antithesis of heavenly Olympus. As fire uplifts, so Woman depresses. Fire in Hesiod is the cooking fire, but latent within fire is the symbolic potential to rep-resent all that constitutes the human spark, intelligence, and culture. John F. Kennedy delivered a stirring example of that symbol in his inaugural address of 20 January 1961: "The energy, the faith, the devotion which we bring to this endeavor will light our country and all who serve it, and the glow from that fire can truly light the world." Woman is identified from the outset in Hesiod's myth-making as the polar opposite of all that defines civilization.

When Zeus chooses the bones covered in fat, he receives something that is good (*kalon*) on the outside but bad (*kakon*) on the inside. Although Hesiod does not say it this way, Zeus gains a *kalon kakon*, a good bad thing. It is bad, not from Zeus's point of view but from that of men who cannot live on bones. Zeus responds to the carving trick and theft of fire by creating Woman. Hesiod calls Woman a *kalon kakon*, a "beautiful ugly thing" or "a good bad thing" (585). She is a retaliation in kind for the useless bones in appetizing fat. Outside, she is a tender maiden, a wonder to behold in beautiful clothes and jewelry of gold. Inside, she is Gaia, here envisioned as worthless dirt. She resembles fire, for both need fuel to survive. The food gained by Prometheus' trick is consumed by Zeus's. Hesiod's Woman is fit to live only with Plenty, not with destructive Poverty (592–93), and the meat obtained by Prometheus' trick goes, in effect, into Woman's stomach. Like the drones in the hive, she remains at ease in the house while men toil to feed her. (No matter that drones are male and fed by sterile female worker bees, Hesiod is not concerned with the facts of bee sexuality.) In his *Works and Days* (302–6), drones are men who do not work and go hungry. Unlike lazy men, however, Woman must be supported even if idle, because the dirt inside her is also Gaia, the soil in which men sow the seed of their sons and heirs.

When Hesiod describes gods and men coming together at Mekone, he uses the common Greek words for mortal men and, undoubtedly, thought of these figures as men. But Woman has yet to be created, and in so far as these "men" are not born of women, they cannot be men. Rather, they are inhabitants of a precivilized state which, to judge from Hesiod's description in a misogynistic tirade on the present, consisted of free association with the gods, freedom from women and work, and the absence of disease, suffering, and death. They resemble the men of the Golden Age in Hesiod's myth of the ages in *Works and Days:*

> The immortal gods who have homes on Olympus made the golden race of mortal men. These men lived like gods during the reign of Kronos with spirits free of cares, far apart from and without toil and woe. Neither did wretched old age come upon them; their hands and feet never changed. Free of all evils, they pleasured in feasts and died as if subdued by sleep.* They had all they needed for living, and the grain-giving field bore them much harvest, unstintingly of its own accord. They lived off their fields as they pleased, at rest among many good things (109–19).

Perhaps the men at Mekone also lived off the earth's spontaneous bounty, but now, with the advent of Woman, they must work the earth for that harvest that once came effortlessly. Moreover, to obtain an heir, they must work the earth that is inside Woman. The analogy of agriculture and marriage is deep-seated in Greek ideology, and the language of one is frequently confounded with that of the other.

Through the story of events at Mekone, Hesiod explains the origin of human existence. By a series of tricks between Zeus and Prometheus consisting of the hiding and stealing of gifts, men receive sacrifice, fire and cooked food, Woman, marriage, and death. These elements of civili-

---

*That men of the Golden Age did not die the death of men born of women is supported by Hesiod's description that "through the plans of great Zeus they are benign spirits over the earth, guardians of mortal men" (*Works and Days* 122–23).

zation act as categories of thought to distinguish the human from the divine and the bestial. The gods do not eat cooked meat but accept the savor rising from the sacrificial fire. Men sacrifice to the gods, eat cooked meat, and, through marriage, restrict their sexual drive. Animals are sacrificed, eat raw meat, and mate promiscuously. Thus, sacrifice, cooked food, and marriage acculturate the pre-civilized male creatures at Mekone, making them human, that is, civilized men.

Before Mekone, there were no oppositions on earth except immortal/mortal. The change is inaugurated by the antithetical nature of Woman, the *kalon kakon* whose inner Gaia is both soil and dirt. Afterwards, the polarity that characterizes human existence comes into being, a polarity that finds expression in the bee simile and in Hesiod's misogynistic outburst, the first such text in Greek literature:

> As when, in hives overhung from above, bees feed drones, participants in evil conspiracies, all day until the setting sun, they busy themselves in packing white honeycombs, while the drones, staying within the sheltered nest, scrape into their stomachs the fruits of another's toil, so high-thundering Zeus ordained women, conspirators in grievous deeds, to be an evil for mortal men. He gave another evil in return for a good. Whoever flees marriage and women's mischievous deeds and chooses not to marry comes to destructive old age without someone [a son] to tend to his old age. He lives in want of nothing, but when he dies, distant relatives divide up his property. For that man whose lot it is to marry and have a trusty wife, one suited to his ways, evil unceasingly rivals good throughout his days. Whoever gets a baneful type [of wife] lives with unremitting sorrow on the spirit and heart in his chest, an evil incurable (594–612).

To see the oppositions in a more concise form:

Men	Women
Worker bees	Drones
Outside	Inside
Poverty	Plenty
Agriculture	Eating another's toil
Toil	Easy life
Old age without an heir	Marriage and an heir

For Hesiod, civilization begins, then, with a breach between men and their gods. Men who sat with the gods openly are now condemned to work and to communicate with the gods through sacrifice. Though they might well resent what Zeus did to them, should that resentment become overt, Zeus could destroy them with his thunderbolt. Hostility does, in fact, break out in the next generation when Zeus tries to wipe out humankind with a flood. The following version of the myth comes from a summary dating from the first or second century A.D. of Apollodorus' *Library*, which was written in the latter part of the second century B.C.

> While king of the territories around Phthia, Deucalion, Prometheus' son, married Pyrrha, the daughter of Epimetheus [Prometheus' brother] and Pandora whom the gods fashioned as the first woman. When Zeus desired that the Bronze Age pass from sight, Deucalion, on Prometheus' advice, built an ark. Loading it with suitable supplies, he embarked with Pyrrha. Zeus poured down from heaven a great deluge and inundated most of Greece so that all mankind perished except for a few who escaped to the nearest high mountains. At that time the mountains in Thessaly separated, and all that lay beyond the Peloponnesus was overwhelmed. Deucalion, carried across the sea in his boat for nine days and as many nights, came to Mt. Parnassus. There, when the downpour stopped, he went out and sacrificed to Zeus of Escapes. Zeus sent Hermes to him and

instructed him to choose what he wanted. Deucalion chose
that there be mankind for him. At Zeus's word, he began
picking up stones and throwing them over his head. Those
which Deucalion threw became men, and those which Pyrrha threw, women. Hence, people were called metaphor-
ically *laoi* from the fact that the word for stone is *laas* (1.7.2).

When the waters recede, Deucalion and Pyrrha sacrifice
to the god, confirming their mortality and human status,
and repopulate the earth by creating men and women.
The transitions demanded in Prometheus' generation have
run their course, and the relationship between gods and
men has been fixed for all time.

Other examples of the myth include Noah in *Genesis* and
Utnapishtim in *The Epic of Gilgamesh*. The latter, known in
antiquity by its first line, "One Who Saw the Abyss," is
believed to have been composed during the Old Babylo-
nian period (c. 2000–1600) from much older versions. A
richly textured work with themes and incidents comparable to those of the Homeric epics, it is preserved in cu-
neiform (wedge-shaped characters on baked clay tablets)
found in the library of Ashurbanipal (eighth century) in
Nineveh. The myth of Utnapishtim's flood is consequently
much older than the *Theogony* or *Genesis*.

Hostility between Zeus and men does not surface in the
generation of Prometheus, because it is diverted away
from Zeus and men onto mediators, Prometheus and
Woman. By mediator, we mean someone or something
that shares qualities of both poles of an opposition but is
not fully identical with either. Being anomalous, a mediator may succeed in overcoming the opposition. Paradise,
for example, serves as a mediator to resolve in part the
opposition of life and death, since it is a place where one
has everlasting life but which can only be reached by dying
in this world. The scout on the American frontier, first
depicted by James Fenimore Cooper in his *Leatherstocking*

Tales, shares the knowledge of the wilderness with the Indian and the culture of the European with the colonist or settler. Neither Indian nor European, the scout functions on the margin between the two. Prometheus is a god, but unlike Olympian Zeus, he is a Titan; like men, he suffers, but, unlike them, he is able to endure unchanged. Chained to a crag, his liver consumed daily by an eagle, he absorbs Zeus's anger. Since he is immortal, his liver regenerates during the night, and hostility is diffused without harming men. Men harbor no resentment toward Prometheus for his trickery, because he acted long ago in the time of first beginnings and because they are in no danger of losing fire. As mediator, Woman shares in the divine in that she is made by the gods; in a way, she is Zeus's daughter. As the origin of "female women" (590), she shares the suffering of men's lives more fully than any creature, despite Hesiod's vituperation. His outcry sufficiently illustrates Woman's role as mediator: it is better to rail at her than at high-thundering Zeus. Moreover, men continue to suffer, and women live with them as constant reminders of things lost. Hesiod's Woman does not remain a mediator but, through her human reincarnations, becomes a scapegoat on whom men ever heap their indignation for what their god did to them.

Men's strategy of attributing and blaming human miseries on Woman is not peculiar to Hesiod. In *Genesis*, Eve gives Adam the fruit of the tree of knowledge of good and evil. He accepts, causing his expulsion from Eden and from the presence of his Lord God. The land now begrudges Adam his bread. The conceptions of paradise and divinity differ, and, unlike Hesiod's Woman, Eve is also punished, yet identical strategies are used to relieve tension. The serpent, comparable as a mythic mediator to Prometheus, receives the brunt of the Lord God's wrath, while Eve survives in her descendants who endure the wrath of men. In *The Epic of Gilgamesh*, Enkidu, child of the mountain, is acculturated by a prostitute. After lying with her for six days and seven nights, he can no longer run with the gazelles, and they flee from him. His body holds him back, marking his separation from the animal or prehuman state. Enkidu now knows what a woman does, and he becomes, in her words, "like a god" [Gardner and Maier, p. 78]. The prostitute clothes him and gives him bread and wine, the food of the man he has become. She brings him to Gilgamesh's city, Uruk, where he encounters Gilgamesh, and, after a brief wrestling match which he loses, the two men embrace in loving friendship. Later, the dying Enkidu curses the prostitute, but the god Shamash reminds him of the benefits he received because of her—"food of the gods," "drink of kings," "a great garment," and the companionship of Gilgamesh who will cause the people to weep for him [Gardner and Maier, pp. 173–79]. Appeased, Enkidu balances his curse with a blessing, acknowledging those goods in the evil of lost freedom.

Hesiod attempts to resolve the problems confronting a ruler of the cosmos by grounding Zeus's rule on the unrealized potential of the past. Zeus frees the Cyclopes from the bonds put upon them by their father Ouranos who "delighted in his evil deed" (158) and did not recognize their value. They, in turn, forge the thunderbolt which they give to Zeus in gratitude. Relying upon it, Zeus is lord of gods and men. At Gaia's prompting, Zeus also releases from bondage the Hundred-Handers whom Ouranos, envying their excessive manliness, beauty, and size, has bound in chains beneath Gaia. With their aid, Zeus acquires the force he needs to subdue the Titans. These sons of the past overwhelm the Titans by hurling three hundred rocks at a time. Zeus then shuts Kronos and the Titans away in the dark, dank mist of Tartarus, where the Hundred-Handers will serve as their guards. In this way, Zeus rids the world of the monstrous Hundred-Handers while he rewards them for their services, proving himself a civilizing and just god.

Zeus's battle for kingship neither takes place within the family nor is directed against the female and her procreativity. Victory alone elevates Zeus above the vengeance owed his father for what he did to him, for no one now has the power to exact retribution from Zeus. Having disclosed to Zeus the means of victory over the Titans, Gaia produces Typhoeus to displace the triumphant Zeus. (This does not fail to surprise, since in all other instances of contact between them, Gaia has succored Zeus.) Typhoeus is a monster from whose shoulders grow a hundred snake heads, out of which come horrible sounds. Had not "the father of men and gods keenly noticed" (838), Typhoeus would have usurped kingship and plunged the cosmos into confusion and chaos, a chaos symbolized by the cacophony of his countless voices [Detienne and Vernant, 1978, p. 117]. "Leaping from Olympus, [Zeus] smote Typhoeus and burned the dreadful monster's wondrous heads" (855–56).

The episode belongs to the theme of Kingship in Heaven, found throughout Mesopotamia in separate versions and different languages. No one version is the source of another; mythmakers adapt the theme to their own objectives and cultures. Some scholars believe that the Typhoeus section was not composed by Hesiod but added later. Such disputes, once begun, rarely are conclusively settled. Nevertheless, the episode shows more openly than any other the latent tension in Hesiod's universe between Gaia and Zeus. Zeus wins kingship by defeating his father and retains it by overcoming Typhoeus, but in both battles Zeus's thunderbolts scorch Gaia. Against the Titans, it is "the life-bearing *gaia*":

> Zeus could no longer hold back his fighting spirit,
> which straightway surged to fill his heart
> and showed all his strength, as from the sky and from
>   Olympos
> he advanced with steady pace amid flashes of lightning

and from his stout hand let fly thunderbolts
that crashed and spewed forth a stream of sacred flames.
The life-giving earth burned and resounded all over
and the vast forest groaned, consumed by fire (687–94;
    Athanassakis, p. 30);

and in the battle against Typhoeus, it is "vast *gaia*":

Then, when Zeus's blows had whipped him to
    submission,
Typhoeus collapsed, crippled, on the groaning giant
    earth
and the flame from the thunder-smitten lord
leaped along the dark and rocky woodlands
of the mountain, and the infernal blast of the flames
set much of the giant earth on fire until it melted (857–
    62; Athanassakis, p. 34).

References to forests clearly foster the image of the earth as the ground, so that most translators concur with Apostolos Athanassakis in not capitalizing the word earth. Yet, when Gaia is set ablaze, the goddess is being punished as well as the ground being burned. The second battle underscores this, for Typhoeus is the son of Gaia born to replace Zeus. All that Zeus is is contained within Gaia, and all that he becomes is given by or taken from her. The antithesis of Zeus, she remains beyond his power, the only figure in Hesiod's universe to do so. Nor can Hesiod have Zeus overcome Gaia directly. How could he? She is the very ground on which the farmer walks and the fertility on which he depends. Through language which misdirects by emphasizing the physical (earth) rather than the cosmic (Gaia), Hesiod vents and exposes the tension between Gaia and Zeus. As in the Prometheus episode, language, the stuff of myths, mediates hostilities that might otherwise destroy the individual and rupture the social fabric.

Force makes Zeus king. Nevertheless, on Gaia's advice,

the Olympian gods urge him to be their king and lord. Zeus distributes to them their spheres of power. Hesiod evidently feels the need to live in a cosmos governed not by violence but by justice. He displaces the violent underpinnings of Zeus's rule onto other beings such as the Hundred-Handers and the children of the river Styx. In the genealogies, children usually resemble their parents in some way; Styx's, however, are utterly different from her. They are Zelos (Object of Envy), Nike (Victory), Kratos (Power), and Bia (Violence). Hesiod confers these qualities upon Zeus indirectly in a myth of his own invention. He explains that Styx alone of the gods fought beside the Olympians against the Titans. Zeus grants her the privileges that the gods will swear unimpeachable oaths by her waters and that her children will always dwell with him. They provide Zeus with the attributes he needs to rule without compromising his position as chosen ruler.

"Zeus, now king, made Metis, who knew the most among gods and mortals, his first wife" (886–87). Only once before does Hesiod put sexual intercourse into the context of marriage: "Perses brought [Asteria] into his great house to be called his wife, and she conceived and gave birth to Hecate" (409–11). Through marriage, the husband and father in Greek patriarchy acculturated the woman's procreativity and turned it to his advantage by producing a son and heir. Hesiod incorporates Hecate into Zeus's patriarchy by having her born in wedlock and relegating her to perpetual virginity [Arthur, 1982, pp. 68–69]. Receiving her powers from the primal division among the Titans, Hecate affords Zeus's Olympian world benefits handed on from the past. With a portion of the earth, the sea, and the heavens as her own, she aids men and acts as an unthreatening mediator between Zeus and humans. She functions actively among humans, particularly in her care for the rearing of male children. In this, she is another example of Hesiod's strategy of fragmenting the female.

Situated among lowly mortals, Hecate is isolated from the society of Olympus. She is the divine counterpart of the unwed daughter secluded in her father's house. Again, we see how cosmogonic myths draw upon everyday reality.

Zeus marries Metis who conceives Athena. When Athena is about to be born, Zeus seduces Metis through deceit and puts her down into his stomach/womb. Gaia's deception of Kronos with the rock and Zeus's outwitting of Prometheus show how important cunning is for a cosmic sovereign. Zeus's cunning, his *dolos*, recalls the cunning of Gaia's scheme against Ouranos; the god, with the advice of Gaia and Ouranos, turns female trickery against the clever Metis. Unlike his predecessors, he devises a stratagem that harmonizes with the birth process. Ouranos tries to stop that process, while Kronos wants to nullify it. Zeus allows the inevitable, the birth of Athena, but escapes its consequences by appropriating the birth process. Athena, born from his head, represents the subordination of the female to the male in the form of the daughter to the father, while Metis remains hidden and imprisoned within Zeus. Zeus thereby acquires her nature which, from her name, is wiliness and resourcefulness of a kind that upsets the status quo. Metis now advises Zeus alone. The contest over sovereignty among the males is ended, since his son by Metis, the only male who could surpass him in cunning and seize kingship, is never conceived. More importantly, the twin threats of the female are finally quelled as Zeus assimilates her deceitful trickery and her procreativity by giving birth to Athena himself.

Hesiod creates out of words a picture of the cosmos in which the problematics of life on earth are held in suspension. Zeus, although he overcomes or escapes the obstacles to his sovereignty, still owes vengeance to his father. The "otherness" of the female has been reduced to its most harmless form in the virgin daughter, yet

Gaia, the primal female, abides. Those in Hesiod's audience might, we suppose, have found release from the hardships imposed by Zeus through the poet's song of male supremacy.

Three

The *Aretē* Standard as a Source of Mythmaking

More than other ancient peoples of the Mediterranean, the Greeks told stories about heroes, the mortal sons of gods and women. Some they placed in the earliest times when monstrous beasts plagued the earth and the cultivated fields of men. Others, later and lesser men, fought around Troy for the return of Helen of Sparta. Uniting the myths of both generations of heroes is the moment of combat against beast or warrior in a life-and-death struggle to win glory. In this chapter we look at how myths validate and criticize what Arthur W.H. Adkins [pp. 31–36] calls the *"aretē* standard." *Aretē* denotes excellence in performing a function. The *aretē* of a knife is measured by its sharpness rather than its studded handle, and the *aretē* of a ship by its swift response in battle. For the warrior, *aretē* meant, first and foremost, prowess in battle or, specifically, the capacity to kill an opponent. Simonides of Chios (c. 556–468) voices the values of the warrior's code in this epitaph composed for the Athenians who fell fighting the Persians at Plataea (479):

> If to die nobly holds the greatest meed of excellence,
>   fortune hath blessed us above all others.
> We strove to bestow freedom upon Greece and lie here
>   enjoying ageless praise (*Greek Anthology* 6.253).

The warrior strove to be best (*aristos*). He vied in intense competition with other *aristoi* to win the most glory possible and to stand out from the group. Admired and rewarded by his community for his bravery, he was expected to be successful in battle and, as the obligation of his bravery, to protect those unable to defend themselves. Nothing excused failure; victory was all. The consequences for his dependents and the women and children of the community—pillage, rape, death, or slavery—were too terrible for them to tolerate less. But the *aretē* standard is flawed, since it generates men whose motives for defending the community engender motives for destroying it. However essential to the survival of his household and the community, the warrior's role situates him on the margin of both. He alone among men is defined by death. At the risk of his life, he fights to save the community not for its sake but for his own. In pursuit of fame, he leaves his household defenseless to enter the battlefield before the city's walls or, in times of peace, the walls of other cities [Redfield, 100–3]. His drive for individual glory not only endangers his own life and that of his family but may spill over into bitter rivalries for primacy with other *aristoi*, imperiling the community from within. These exemplars of the *aretē* standard fill the lines of heroic or epic poetry.

The greatest of the epic poets is Homer. Greeks generally believed that Homer composed both the *Iliad* and the *Odyssey*; although there was no unanimity of opinion about where he lived or when, they accepted that there was a man called Homer. Modern views of Homer are vastly different. In 1795, Friedrich August Wolf in his *Prolegomena ad Homerum* contended that the Homeric poems were not written by the same man, nor was each poem written by a single poet. Convinced that without the aid of writing no one artist could compose either so long a work or one so well constructed, Wolf maintained that the poems, composed around 950, were a conflation of short songs assembled by compilers and editors and preserved through memory until written down in the sixth century. Wolf's thesis ignited the fury of the Homeric Question. The "Analysts" scrutinized the poems for inconsistencies and mistakes, hoping to uncover the telltale evidence for Wolf's "editors." "Unitarians" fought back, insisting on the unity of authorship but failing to agree on a description of that unity. Their debate preoccupied Homeric scholarship until the mid–1930s, when Milman Parry's theories of Homeric composition gained attention [Adam Parry]. Parry proposed that the two epics were the product of many poets who did not compose pen in hand but rather sang before audiences, using traditional phrases (formulas) put together extemporaneously to the accompaniment of a single-stringed instrument. Formulas such as "man-slaying Hector" or "godlike Odysseus" had been created by countless singers over generations, helping bards to express the recurring situations and themes of epic poetry. Parry further explained that variations and inconsistencies in the poems might well have resulted from the bard's changing emphasis on particular matters or, given the extemporaneity of his performance, from mistakes. An audience of listeners would not notice or would not care whether the Greek wall in the *Iliad* was always in the same place or whether it sometimes disappeared (as it does). Scholars have since modified Parry's conception of the formula, but his observation that the composer or, more likely, the composers were oral poets remained unshaken for more than fifty years, when his methodology and consequently his concept of the oral bard began to be challenged [Shive]. But Parry's very thesis clearly left many questions unanswered and rendered it no simple matter to talk about Homer. As a result of his conclusions, anything said about the poet himself has to be considered speculative. Who, then, was Homer, and if the poems were composed to be heard, how and by whom were they written down? One tradition from earliest times identifies Homer as a man from Chios, an island off the Ionian coast; although the preponderance of Ionic Greek in the extant epics suggests that Homer and other bards lived in Ionia, no definitive answers to these questions are ever likely to emerge.

In any event, for our purposes, Homer is the source of the extant versions of the *Iliad* and the *Odyssey;* he is the "monumental" poet, the one who, deeply imbued with the oral techniques of heroic poetry, also knew how to go beyond the limitations of traditional methods and material. He gave lasting form to one version of "the wrath of Achilles" and "the homecoming of Odysseus," both of which had been sung in other ways by other poets. This feat was accomplished because the version of the "monumental" poet (or poets) was written down, achieving the permanence of the written record. The mechanics of that process are lost in time.

The method scholars once conjured of Homer singing to a scribe, if that ever did occur, was surely not the first form of recording. The alphabet entered the Greek world around 720, but literacy spread slowly and sporadically. Eric A. Havelock [1982, pp. 179–81] has suggested that a few verses were written down first as prompters and aids to memory. Oral poets, dependent upon their memories, might eagerly take advantage of a new technique that eased their burden. From that beginning, longer and longer transcriptions were made until sufficient skill had been acquired to accommodate poems of the length of the *Iliad* and the *Odyssey*.

The singer, chanting to his lyre, created the first medium of heroic poetry. He made a world of words, one that had never existed but that his audience and the poet himself believed real and historical, for it had the authority of the past. Odysseus therefore praises Demodokos not for the pleasure he received from his singing but for its accuracy.

Demodokos, you I laud above all mortals. The Muse, daughter of Zeus, or Apollo taught you, for you sing the ruin of the Achaeans in exceedingly good order, what the Achaeans accomplished and endured and what they suffered, as if you yourself were present or had heard from another who was (*Odyssey* 8.487–91).

There could be no higher praise for the poet.

Some poets, like Homer's Phemios and Demodokos, lived at the court of a baron; others wandered from city to city. The respect afforded them was comparable to that granted heralds and other artisans. They were professionals, superior by virtue of their experiences and craft, who related events and sang words revealed and given to them by the goddess, the Muse. Thus, the suitors' coercion of Phemios, "who sang among the suitors out of necessity" (*Odyssey* 1.154), must be read as another sign of the impudence which makes them overlook the possibility of Odysseus' return. The *Odyssey* also provides a detailed description that reflects the regard in which bards were held.

The herald approached, leading the trusty singer, him whom the Muse loved and gave a good and an evil; she took away his sight but gave him sweet song. Pontonoös set out a chair studded with silver for him in the midst of the feasters, leaning it against the great pillar. The herald then hung the clear-toned lyre from a peg above his head and showed him how to take it into his hands. He put a beautiful table beside him, bread, and a goblet of wine, for when the spirit bid him to drink. The feasters reached out for the food spread ready before them. When they put aside desire for eating and drinking, the Muse stirred the singer to sing the accomplishments of men from the poem whose fame reached broad heaven, the quarrel of Odysseus and Peleus' son Achilles when they quarreled with direful

words at the bounteous feast of the gods, and lord of men
Agamemnon took joy because the best of the Achaeans
were wrangling (8.62–78).

Had we Demodokos' song, we would have received background, heard impassioned, angry speeches, and come to
understand the men involved—all from listening to the
bard.

In a culture where literacy remained rare long after the
introduction of writing, oral poets were the repositories of
the past. Epic poems were many and lost with the ephemerality of the spoken word, but if individual renditions of
an incident such as the quarrel of Odysseus and Achilles
vanished, the quarrel itself would be remembered as long
as there were poets endowed with their craft and audiences willing to learn their songs. To us, as students of
Greek mythology, it cannot matter that the poet was not
bound by events that took place in the "real" world, for
his songs nonetheless contain the beliefs, tensions, con-
flicts, and ethics of a culture we seek to understand.

There were other media for heroic poetry besides the
songs of the professional bard. As might well be expected,
amateurs, too, tried their hand at the art. In *Iliad 9*, the
embassy sent from Agamemnon finds Achilles singing the
"deeds of men" for his own amusement and that of his
friend Patroklos (189–90). Guilds were organized whose
members recited the poems from memory. Whether the
guild members were creative poets themselves is contro-
versial. In the mid-sixth century, Pisistratus, tyrant of Athens (546–527), added Homeric recitations to the Great
Panathenaeic festival in an attempt to associate Athens
with the Greek triumphs of the past and to promote its
leadership in Ionia. Rhapsodes, or "stitchers of songs,"
competed with other rhapsodes. By the late fifth century,
rhapsodes, distinguished by their brightly colored robes,
could be heard nearly every day on the streets of Athens.

Athenians were also reminded of the Trojan War and other incidents drawn from Homer by vase paintings, statues, and such monumental art as the Parthenon. But the most pervasive medium was the spoken word of the people themselves. Teachers drilled their students in Homer, for memory of the poems defined the educated man. Older men tested one another's command of the poems in competitions and performances at private and public feasts and rituals.

In manifold ways, Greeks kept the Homeric tradition alive and absorbed its moral and behavioral precepts. It was no mundane past that the bards recalled but the acts of gods and heroes. By their words and deeds, the heroes established a model for bravery, obedience, endurance, and manliness, implicitly prescribing it for lesser men. The singer was neither philosopher nor teacher in any formal sense, but his heroes showed men how to act for good or evil by their example, and his stories had the power of a living reality.

How the Homeric poems functioned as a source of precedents may be seen in the epics themselves. Achilles, for example, recounts the story of Niobe in the last book of the *Iliad* in order to persuade Priam to pause in his grief for his son Hector, at least long enough to take nourishment. In the *Odyssey*, the story of Orestes' slaying Aegisthus, the murderer of his father Agamemnon, is more than once evoked to urge Telemachus to slay the suitors who are disrupting and despoiling the household of his absent father Odysseus. With Hector dead and Odysseus' whereabouts unknown, the responsibility for restoring order falls to a father and a son, respectively, and it is as appeals for the restoration of order that Niobe's and Orestes' stories are told.

On a wider scale, the poet of the *Iliad* effects order in the army after Agamemnon, the king and focus of society's religious and political unity, quarrels with Achilles, its foremost warrior and focus of society's need for fighters; and, in the *Odyssey*, he reestablishes order in the family by bringing the husband and master back to the house-hold. The plot in both instances traces the hero's separa-tion from society, the slaughter and suffering that result, and redress and renewal upon his return. Achilles with-draws from the fighting; Greeks and Achilles' companion Patroklos are slain; Achilles returns, and "all the Achaeans were in one body together" (*Iliad* 19.54). Odysseus, leaving Troy, is blown off course and wanders in a never-never land; his crew perishes, and suitors of his wife invade and pillage his house; Odysseus comes back to Ithaca, slays the suitors, and is reintegrated into his household. The same movement (out and back) recurs within each epic, constituting its overall plot. That plot, in turn, repeatedly portrays social dysfunction as the inevitable consequence of behavioral deviation and disorder.

To the Greek poet addressing a patriarchal society whose men were reared to be warriors and therefore necessarily left their families for periods of time, the maintenance of order, whether on the field of battle or in the household, was tantamount to the continuance of society; its absence spelled the end of civilization itself. In fact, heroic poetry seeks on every level to convey that principle. Themes, plot, moral values, rhetorical devices, and even the poet's use of meter manifest the overwhelming importance that he lent to the restoration of order and stability. To illustrate this more fully, we examine in some detail Nestor's edu-cation of Patroklos in *Iliad* 11.

In *Iliad* 9, Achilles rejects Agamemnon's apology for the quarrel and his gifts of compensation. On the next day (*Iliad* 11), the fighting begins anew, but Achilles remains apart from it although watching from his ship. At first the Greeks prevail but, hard-pressed, their leaders withdraw, wounded. Achilles catches sight of Nestor bringing in a wounded man and sends Patroklos to find out his name.

Having learned it is the healer Machaon, Patroklos is anxious to return. The old man, however, detains him and obliges him to listen to his voice of experience. Nestor, so aged that "in his time two generations of mortal men had perished" (1.250–51), tells Patroklos of his past, so long gone that it has acquired the aura of myths. He proceeds to teach the impatient youth what it means to act like a man among men.

In the following quotation Nestor laments the wounding of the heroes. The poet builds the episode line by line, heightening the anguish and horror of the account. In the text below, the Greek has been transliterated, and the quantities of the syllables, long (-) or short (˘), have been marked. A literal translation in the same word order as the Greek follows each line.

655 Tōn d'ēmeībĕt' ĕpēītă Gĕrēnĭŏs hīppŏtă Nēstōr:
Him [Patroklos] answered then Gerenian horseman, Nestor:

656 "tīptĕ t'ăr' hōd' Ăchĭleūs ŏlŏphȳrĕtăī hūĭăs Ăchāīōn,
"Why then does Achilles lament for the sons of Achaeans,

657 hōssōī dē bĕlĕsīn bĕblĕătăī? ōudĕ tī ōĭdĕ
who with missiles have been struck? Not anything does he know

658 pēnthĕŏs, hōssŏn ŏrōrĕ kătā strătŏn; hōī găr ărīstōī
of sorrow, all that goes through the army; for the best men

659 ēn neūsīn kĕătāī bĕblēmĕnŏī ōutămĕnōī tĕ.
in ships lie struck and wounded.

660 bēblētāī mĕn hŏ Tȳdĕĭdēs krătĕrōs Dĭŏmēdēs;
Struck has been the son of Tydeos, strong Diomedes;

661   ōutāstāi d'Ŏdÿsēus dōurīklÿtŏs ēd' Ăgămēmnŏn;
      wounded has been Odysseus, renowned for the
      spear, and Agamemnon;

662   bēblētāi dĕ kăi Eurÿpÿlŏs kătă mērŏn ŏïstōi;
      struck also has been Eurypylos in a thigh by an arrow;

663   tōutōn d'ăllŏn ĕgō nĕŏn ēgăgŏn ēk pŏlĕmōiŏ
      this other I newly brought from battle

664   īŏï ăpō nēurēs bēblēmĕnŏn. āutăr Ăchīllēus. . . ."
      with an arrow from a bowstring struck. But Achil-
      les. . . ."

Each line conforms to a metrical scheme which is repeated
from the beginning, consisting of five dactyls (-~~) and one
spondee (--); a spondee may be substituted for any dactyl,
except the fifth, and the last two syllables, usually a spondee, may be a trochee (-~). Alternatives between dactyls
and spondees occur throughout the line, but the pattern
becomes more fixed and regular as the line approaches the
end. In this passage, the last three feet, except in the tro-
chaic lines 657, 659, and 663, are identical: dactyl, dactyl,
spondee. Words which change least, such as proper
names, also occur more commonly at the end of the line.
Thus, the transition from uncertainty to certainty is re-
played through sound again and again as each line is sung.

The repetition and placement of the word for "struck"
drive home the full horror of the scene produced by
Achilles' withdrawal from the battle. Forms of the verb
ballō (to strike as with a missile) appear five times in these
ten lines, three times at the end of the fourth foot followed
by a pause, and twice in the emphatic position at the beginning of the line. The latter sequence in particular creates
an image of the heaping up of the dead and wounded. In
each instance of its use, the word occupies more than one

foot, and its very length amplifies its sound which imitates that of an arrow striking its target. In the last line, Homer reverses the natural quantities of the second and fourth syllables so that a break occurs after the long participle *beblēmenon*. Although such a pause followed by the sound pattern of *autar Achilleus* is formulaic in so far as both appear in this position in other lines of the *Iliad*, it is important to observe that the break here not only marks the end of the account of the wounding but places final emphasis on the disastrous results of Achilles' wrath.

The reproach against Achilles resumes:

> But Achilles, though brave, does not care for the Danaans nor pity them. Is he actually waiting until the swift ships beside the sea grow warm with the hostile fire, with the Argives standing by helpless, and we ourselves perish one after another? O, that strength were in my bent limbs as before (11.664–69).

By way of contrast, Nestor describes at length how he acted as a young man when a dispute over cattle-rustling erupted between his people from Pylos and the Epeians of neighboring Elis. That was the time, he says, when he killed his first man, Itymoneus, son of brave Hypeirochos. (Details such as these attest to the accuracy of the poet's song.) Itymoneus was struck by a javelin from Nestor's hand while both fought in the front of their armies. The Pylians took countless spoils, collecting the debts owed them and avenging outrages inflicted by the Epeians. "Neleus [Nestor's father] was joyful because many things befell me who went to the fighting so young" (683–84). When the Epeians counterattacked, and Neleus would have his son remain behind, Nestor went out as a footman among the cavalry.

> From there we armed with all speed and came at noon with our weapons to the sacred stream of Alpheios. There we

sacrificed fine victims to almighty Zeus, a bull to Alpheios
and another to Poseidon, but to gray-eyed Athena, a cow
from the herds. Then we took dinner throughout the army
in our companies, and we slept, each man in his armor,
beside the streams of the sea. But the great-spirited Epeians
surrounded the town, eager to ravage it. A great deed of
Ares stood revealed before us. When the gleaming sun
towered over the earth we joined in battle (725–36).

The old man continues his tale, telling of the many he slew
and of the plunder he seized. Then he closes the account
of his past as he had begun it—with a reference to
Achilles—as if to emphasize the lesson Patroklos must
learn: "But Achilles will enjoy his bravery alone; truly, I
think that he will weep much after the people are killed"
(762–64).

Nestor now turns to Patroklos' past, reminding the
young man of what was said on the day that Achilles'
father Peleus entertained Odysseus and Nestor. They had
come to gather men for the expedition against Troy and
to fetch Achilles and Patroklos who yearned to get into
the fight. Menoitios, Patroklos' father, urged his son to
advise and counsel Achilles. " 'He will be persuaded,' "
quotes Nestor, " 'to the better.' Thus the old man enjoined upon you, but you have forgotten" (789–90). With
faint hope that Patroklos may sway Achilles back into the
fighting, Nestor makes his request: let Achilles send Patroklos into battle dressed in Achilles' armor and followed
by his people. Patroklos' death the next day ends Achilles'
withdrawal but initiates a new, more drastic separation,
that of Achilles from all that defines the human. Homer
thus builds a complex and value-laden narrative on variations of a limited number of themes. His Nestor, like the
poet himself, is an educator of values. The old warrior
shows Patroklos by the example of his own youth the
meaning of manhood. His encounter with the Epeians

demonstrates that a man must fight among his fellows, out in front, and face to face with the enemy. That is the place where the joy that a young man can give his father is won; that is the place of wealth, vengeance, and proven bravery. On the other hand, the scene in Peleus' house illustrates the obedience that the young should grant their elders. Patroklos has forgotten; Nestor reminds him not only to obey his father and counsel Achilles but to comply with the request of the old man sitting before him.

Achilles' withdrawal perverts the normal expectations of the fighting, since the Trojans slaughter the stronger Greeks. Nestor tries to reverse this situation by bringing Achilles back with the message of values that past success confirmed as right: my behavior was proper then and ought to be taken by you, younger men, as the way you should act now. Had Achilles heeded the wisdom of the past and not withheld his bravery, he would not have suffered the loss of his friend. In particular, this episode exemplifies how heroic poetry seeks to restore order, for heroic poetry prescribes fitting behavior and, within the confines of its verse, implies as a reward the maintenance of the status quo.

For Nestor, the warrior's life is social. A man joins others because they recognize his worth and confer upon him the prizes of combat and the glory of success. Nestor puts his message in the context of what every son assumed— to be better than his father—and what every father ex-pected—to be obeyed by his son. The dynamic subordi-nates individual prowess and youth to community and age, blatantly contradicting the reality experienced by the warrior himself. The Lycian Sarpedon, in answering his own question to his friend Glaukos, gives the warrior's reasons for fighting:

> Glaukos, why are we two most held in honor with place at table, meat, and more cups in Lycia, and all men look

upon us as gods, and we possess a large portion of land along the banks of the Xanthos good for orchards and fields of wheat? Now among the foremost of the Lycians we must stand and meet the burning battle so someone of the armed Lycians may say: "Surely, no ignoble kings of ours rule throughout Lycia and eat the fattened flocks and drink the choice honey-sweet wine. Their might is good since they fight among the foremost Lycians." Fool. If, escaping this war, we would remain ever ageless and immortal, I myself would not fight nor would I send you into the fight that glorifies a man. Now, as it is, the spirits of death stand about us, countless. No mortal can flee or avoid them. Let us go and offer our boast to someone or he to us (12.310–28).

The warrior seeks combat among the foremost fighters where his *aretē* may be seen and his boast to be the best at something may be proven. He fights to attain the respect that brings honor and material gains and softens the inevitability of death. Through fighting he becomes like a god among men and achieves the mediated immortality of his culture, remembrance through songs like Homer's. But men are not gods, and all men die. Unlike the majority, however, the warrior chooses to die on his own terms for honor. Such is Sarpedon's insight into the *aretē* standard, and such is his reason for "boasting."

In *Iliad* 1, the pretense of the *aretē* standard that honor attested to by gifts compensates for the loss of life comes home to Achilles in a devastating insight. When Agamemnon, king and repository of social norms, must forfeit his prize, he demands another, and Achilles explodes:

O clothed in shamelessness, ever bent on profit, how will any of the Achaeans readily obey you either to go on a journey or to fight with strength against men? (149–51).

His reproach is addressed less to Agamemnon himself, a "strong spearfighter," than to the community for which

the king stands. Out of the diffidence that marks his character, Agamemnon makes a mistake. By demanding back
rather than distributing prizes, he undermines the foundation of his power. Prizes, awards above the common
division, confirm by their existence the warrior's *aretē* and
substantiate his worth and honor among the fighters. Consequently, they are valued not only for their intrinsic worth
but also for the high social estimation they confer. When
Agamemnon takes back Achilles' prize, the woman Briseis, he deprives him of the token of those qualities that
made life worthwhile and imparted meaning to it. By his
action, Agamemnon reduces gifts to mere objects of
wealth, to possessions emptied of the mystique that transmits quality to life [Schein, p. 106]. Achilles, acute with
the narrow vision of the self-consumed, perceives what
Agamemnon has done, reviles the king as if he were a
merchant seeking profits, and storms out of the council.
When Agamemnon later appeals with many fine gifts for
him to return to the battle, Achilles refuses. He no longer
values them as embodiments of honor. Richmond Lattimore's translation [p. 206] aptly captures the essence of
his refusal:

> Fate is the same for the man who holds back, the same if
>   he fights hard.
> We are all held in a single honour, the brave with the
>   weaklings.
> A man dies still if he has done nothing, as one who has
>   done much (*Iliad* 9.318–20).

Achilles' are powerful words, expressing in staccato total
rejection of the *aretē* standard. For him, prizes no longer
erect the differences between men that induce the warrior
to enter mortal combat. His spleen inflamed by his quarrel
with Agamemnon, he sits in his camp stultified, unable
to find the quality to live by in his culture's values or in

himself. The ensuing verses allow Homer to reach closure for Achilles' wrath and impose an aura of order upon the universe.

The quarrel between Achilles and Odysseus that Demodokos sings before the Phaeacians may have belonged to the epic tradition, posing the question: would Troy be taken by the might of Achilles or by the strategems of Odysseus [Nagy, pp. 45–47]? But no version of it remains. Even so, the contrast between the response of each hero to the demands of the *aretē* standard appears striking enough to have generated the theme. Achilles acts through force; his fighting, he boasts, will be missed by the sons of the Achaeans when Hector slaughters them in their numbers. Odysseus acts characteristically through artifice or shiftiness, the quality Hesiod identifies with the goddess Metis. Homer's common epithets for Odysseus, "much-suffering" and "of many ways," mark his endurance and readiness in devising schemes. In his encounter with Scylla and Charybdis in *Odyssey 12*, Odysseus arms himself to face the goddess Scylla's attack which he cannot forfend. While martial force fails, and would again on his return through the clashing rocks, he survives Charybdis by contrivance and suffering:

> I was carried along through the night, and at dawn I came to Scylla's crag and the dread Charybdis who was sucking in the sea's salty water. But I hung from a great fig tree overhead and held on, clinging to it like a bat. There was no place to prop my feet or to stand on. The roots were far from me, and the branches towered above overshadowing Charybdis. I held on constantly until it vomited back the mast and keel. They came late to me though I longed for them. When a man rises up from the marketplace for dinner after judging many disputes of litigious young men, then did the beams appear from Charybdis. I let go my feet and hands and fell down between the long timbers. Sitting on them, I rowed with my hands. The

father of men and gods did not let Scylla see me, for I
would not have escaped sheer destruction (429–46).

The episode illustrates Odysseus' wit and strength to per-
severe in hardship, in a word, the *aretē* necessary for him
to win his life and homecoming. The implied simile of the
marketplace highlights his judgment, here put to compre-
hending the rhythm of the whirlpool, and evokes the goal
of his suffering, Penelope, who, were he home in Ithaca,
would be overseeing his dinner.

Achilles vents his rage upon Hector for slaying Patroklos
and for his own failure to stand by his friend. His violence
in fighting wins honor for him among the Argives when
he is alive. And, as Odysseus tells him in the underworld,
"you have great power among the dead" (*Odyssey* 11.485–
86). But Achilles' well-known reply undermines the values
of the *aretē* standard, which he had exemplified in life and
which led to his death:

> I would rather be a field hand serving another for hire, a
> man without portion himself who has little livelihood, than
> be lord for all the dead departed (489–91).

For Homer of the *Odyssey* another imperative takes precedence. The warrior must live to return home. However
much society depends upon fighters, it cannot survive
unless its men come back to be husbands and fathers.
Upon leaving Troy, Odysseus and his men attack the
Kikonians:

> There I sacked their city and slew them. Taking their wives
> and many possessions from the city, we divided them up
> so that none went without his fair share (9.40–42).

The incident, typical of the Trojan War, epitomizes the
Greek invaders' attitude toward women as property and

prizes of battle. A supernatural storm afterwards veers Odysseus off course and impels him into a realm dominated by forces representing nature. He cannot subject the goddesses and other females he encounters to his will nor overcome by physical strength the might of the sea or Polyphemos. The wanderings permit Homer to bring home to Ithaca not the man who plundered Troy and the Kikonians but the man who, by the time he reaches the Phaeacians, can weep for the women of a sacked city.

In his treatise *On the Fame of Athenians*, Plutarch (c. A.D. 50–c. 120) preserves an observation by the fifth-century sophist and rhetorician Gorgias (c. 483–376) of Leotini in Sicily:

> Tragedy flourished and was proclaimed as a wondrous and delightful sound and spectacle of men of old accomplishing through myths and emotions a "deception," as Gorgias says, "in which the deceiver is more just than the one who does not deceive, and the deceived wiser than the one not deceived." For the deceiver is more just because, making a promise, he fulfills it, but the deceived is wiser because, through the pleasure of words, the unperceived is easily captured (fr. 23).

Plutarch embeds the quotation from Gorgias in explanatory material of his own. How much he is indebted to his source for Gorgias is unknown, but his comments are nonetheless useful for beginning our study of tragedy as another mythic medium exploiting the *aretē* standard.

Meager traces remain of the place where Aeschylus (525/4–456), Sophocles (c. 496–406), and Euripides (c. 485–c. 406) staged their dramas. Once their theater housed sights and sounds whose impact upon their audiences was immediate. Actors' voices and songs and the rhythmic motions of the chorus stirred and shaped the emotions of those watching and listening. The biography included in the manuscripts of the tragedian Aeschylus claims that when the Erinyes in the *Eumenides* (458) ran pell-mell onto the stage, the weak expired and women miscarried (*Life of Aeschylus* 9). Hyperbolic as the account seems, it is not impossible that some in the audience confused the representation with the reality. Gorgias considered tragedy a form of rhetoric because of its emotive force. In tragedy, the persuasive power of the spoken word works a deception upon the listeners. Rhetoric has the same effect, Gorgias believed, because most men, ignorant of events, rely upon opinion and can therefore be manipulated. The unscrupulous orator takes advantage of their ignorance to mislead them, but the tragedian deceives without being dishonest, because he instructs his audience and makes them wiser. They hear the ineffable and behold the suppressed about their society and themselves. The words of the tragedian's myths, transformed by his medium, do not seek order in the same way as the bard's. Rather, they unsettle complacency and confront the beliefs they uphold.

The god of tragedy, Dionysus, came from Eleutherae on the border of Attica and Boeotia. His advent at Athens probably happened when Pisistratus integrated the Eleutherians into Attica, and so the god is called Dionysus Eleuthereus. The move afforded the people of a small town protection against their Boeotian neighbors and furthered Pisistratus' policy of directing the religious loyalties of the people toward the *polis* and himself and away from the hereditary cults of aristocratic families. At first, Athenians worshipped Dionysus in celebrations throughout the Attic countryside. The main rite was a procession conducting sacrificial victims, traditionally bulls, to the god's sanctuary on the southern slope of the Acropolis. The celebrants carried bread shaped into long thin spits, grapes and wine, offerings of the first fruits of the harvest, and phalluses. The procession left from the Academy, a shrine and gymnasium dedicated to the hero Academus, located outside the city on the road to Boeotia. It paused on the way at other shrines and places where dances were offered in honor of the deity. Arriving at Dionysus' precinct, the celebrants immolated the victims and feasted on the god's bounty of beef and cup after cup of wine. Afterwards, those still able went by torchlight into the night to revel in the streets, singing and dancing to the accompaniment of flutes and harps. From such an ordinary beginning, somehow—the evidence does not allow certainty—tragedy developed out of the choral singing and dancing, and the City (or Great) Dionysia became a showcase for Athenian splendor, wealth, and power.

What first comes to mind in thinking of Dionysus is wine, drunken orgies, and lustful satyrs frolicking with willing nymphs, but wine is actually a later manifestation of Dionysus, and tipsy Bacchus derives from poets writing in Egyptian Alexandria after 300. Seldom depicted by the Greeks as intoxicated, Dionysus looms calmly amid the frenzy inspired by his presence. He is the god—the reality—inherent in the realm of liquid nature. By consuming Dionysus in milk, honey, water, wine, or the blood of a freshly slain animal, his worshippers become enthused with him. The god within them, they stand outside of their everyday rational selves and, in this ecstatic state, become themselves Bacchae. All bonds and restraints fallen away, they give themselves over to the animal within.

Dionysus shatters the distinctions that define the human condition, as the myth of his birth illustrates. Apollodorus records this version of his birth:

> Zeus became impassioned for Semele and bedded her unbeknown to Hera. Hera tricked Semele into asking Zeus to do for her whatever she requested. She asked that he come to her as he was when he courted Hera. Unable to refuse, Zeus entered her bedchamber on a chariot with his lightning flashes and crashes of thunder and let loose a

thunderbolt. Semele died of fright, but Zeus snatched up the six-month-old fetus that had aborted from the fire and sewed it into his thigh. . . . In due time, Zeus cut the stitches and gave birth to Dionysus (*Library* 3.4.3).

Had Dionysus been born of Semele, daughter of the Theban Cadmus, he would have been mortal like his mother. Instead, he becomes a god, destroying the barriers dividing mortal from immortal as well as those severing female from male, for the god is sired by a male and delivered from a male.

Dionysus and the madness he ignites merge the individual with the group, the human with the bestial, and the mortal with the immortal. Walter F. Otto captures his essence in a lyrical passage that itself seems enthused with the god's presence:

But the god himself is not merely touched and seized by the ghostly spirit of the abyss. He, himself, is the monstrous creature which lives in the depths. From its mask it looks out at man and sends him reeling with the ambiguity of nearness and remoteness, of life and death in one. Its divine intelligence holds the contradictions together. For it is the spirit of excitation and wildness; and everything alive, which seethes and glows, resolves the schism between itself and its opposite and has already absorbed this spirit in its desire. Thus all earthly powers are united in the god: the generating, nourishing, intoxicating rapture; the life-giving inexhaustibility; and the tearing pain, the deathly pallor, the speechless night of having been. He is the mad ecstasy which hovers over every conception and birth and whose wildness is always ready to move on to destruction and death [pp. 140–41].

The Athenians welcomed into their holiest of holies a deity benevolently antithetical to the order sustaining the city around his temple, one who restores and reinvigorates within the safe confines of the theater the bonds uniting the community through the orgiastic savagery of the wilds.

The audience enters the theater in the early hours of the morning during the month of Elaphebolion (March). They are already excited by the holiday and the release it brings from duties and obligations. Tragedies will be performed for three days, a brief interlude further shortened by the expense of admission. Poorer citizens who have registered have received allowances from state funds for the price of admission. They know what myths the dramatist has chosen and how they end, but they eagerly anticipate seeing how he will treat them. Farmers, craftsmen, shopkeepers, and such outnumber the gentry and intellectuals. Nonetheless, they are an experienced audience; some have participated in the staging of other dramas. They know what to look for and look forward to having their expectations satisfied. They sit on the sloping ground; above the orchestra, there are few, if any seats. Crowded together, they feel the movements and perceive the reactions of one another. Sophocles' *Ajax* begins, and Odysseus walks cautiously on stage. Through the magic of the mask, the actor has disappeared into the hero of times past. His strong, clear-toned voice and exaggerated movements convey the meaning of his words without interrupting the spell. The chorus sing and dance; the rhythmic movements of their feet echo the concern for Ajax voiced in their lyrics. The flute sounds its orgiastic strains, weaving in and around the melody. The viewers, forgetful of themselves, escape into the plight of Ajax. They stand outside themselves in the ecstasy of Dionysus Eleuthereus.

This description, which draws upon W.B. Stanford's study of emotionalism in Greek tragedy [1983], is hypothetical. The scripts do not afford sufficient evidence for the choreography, music, and emotional impact on the audience to say anything for certain. But some notion of how tragedy breaks down the structure of Athenian culture and calls its values, beliefs, and prejudices into question is possible.

In a typical tragedy, the protagonist, in Vernant's term, "debates" the chorus [1970, p. 284; 1980, pp. 195–96]. The protagonist represents a figure from the mythic past, a time far enough ago to be different from but not totally alien to contemporary Athens. That distance must have been reinforced not only by the difference in dress between the hero and chorus, but also by the disparity between the professional actors playing heroes and the amateurs of the chorus playing ordinary people whose outlook concurs with the mores of the *polis*, with belief in unity and social harmony through moderation and subordination to the gods. Offsetting the familiarity of those values are intricately structured rhythms and patterns of phraseology of the lyrics the chorus sings, which are distinct from colloquial speech. The hero, on the other hand, acts in accord with the *aretē* standard, asserting individual eminence over social conformity but speaking in a language similar to normal speech. Together, hero and chorus probe the meaning of his actions from opposing ethical viewpoints, an antithesis heightened by the other contrasts. Whereas the myths of heroes in epic are told to reinforce social integrity, assumed to be valuable for itself, those of tragic heroes, in exposing problems and flaws in the culture, raise questions about the very fabric of society.

The *aretē* standard in its Homeric form was anachronistic by the fifth century. From the eighth century on, a wider distribution of wealth and political power, as well as the weakening of dependence on others, brought change [Forrest, 1966, pp. 67–97], and there emerged the *polis*, a political and religious community of citizens ruled by law. Concomitant with the development of the *polis* was a style of fighting that reflected the principle of subordination of the individual to the whole to insure its survival and prosperity.

The new fighting man wore armor of metal, a breast-plate, helmet, and greaves covering his lower legs, and fought close against other men similarly armed. He was the "man of the shield," the *hoplitēs* or hoplite, named from Greek *hoplon* (shield). The shield he carried was round, about three feet in diameter, and of wood reinforced with bronze. Its distinctive feature was two straps, one in the middle and another on the right rim. The man inserted his left arm in the middle and gripped the outer strap. In this configuration, his right side, free to wield a thrusting spear or sword, remained exposed to the enemy, while the *hoplon* extended to the left beyond his body. The shield made the hoplite dependent for protection upon the man to his right. The safety of all therefore depended on the courage of each man to stand beside the others. "Let the man stand firm," Tyrtaeus (seventh century) exhorts his fellow Spartans, "and remain fixed with both feet on the ground, biting his lips" (fr. 10). The *aretē* of the Homeric/aristocratic warrior is thus transformed into a civic virtue. As Walter Donlan observes,

> It is important to stress that this [recasting] is not so much a rejection of the code of the aristocratic warrior as it is a transvaluation. Essentially the Tyrtaean scheme subsumes all the excellence of the fighting man into the single cause of service to the whole community [p. 43].

And yet *aretē* in its modified form continued to engage Athenians and all Greeks in intense competition for honor. "The zest for competitive struggle that pervades Greek culture finds all manner of expression" [Gouldner, p. 46]. In their competitions, there could be but one winner; all others were losers. Consequently, competitors were inclined to bitter rivalries, to trying to win at any cost, and to breaking the rules if defeat threatened [Gouldner, p. 50]. The same divisiveness is caused by the civic *aretē*.

The Athenians gathered on the slope of the Acropolis were well acquainted with Ajax. He was born the son of Telamon on the island of Salamis off the Attic coast. His exploits in the Trojan War won for him cultic honors both in his homeland and in Attica. Some forty years before (480), Athenians about to engage in a naval battle around Salamis had invoked his aid against the Persians. He was known through epic tradition, particularly Homer's *Iliad*, as the biggest and bravest of the Greeks at Troy after Achilles. "The bulwark of the Achaeans" (3.229), he was marked by his huge shield and excelled in defensive fighting. Despite his prominence, he lost the contest for Achilles' armor, the armor made for Achilles by Hephaestus, which Achilles' mother Thetis offered as a prize for the best Achaean after her son's death. Some attributed Ajax's loss to the Trojans' claim that Odysseus caused them more harm than he did; others put the responsibility on Athena, who felt that Odysseus' wiliness would injure the hated Trojans more than Ajax's brawn. What would Sophocles say about the contest? He could hardly ignore it, since the contest precipitated Ajax's death by suicide.

In *Ajax*, produced in the mid-440s, Sophocles explores the destructive potential of the civic *aretē* through the historically removed figures of Homeric *aristoi*, particularly Ajax as son of a warrior [Tyrrell, 1985, pp. 179–84]. Every man was expected to surpass his father in deeds and fame. Competition allowed the household to prosper, while the father's age precluded open rivalry from breaking out. Sthenelos' reply to Agamemnon in *Iliad* 4 illustrates the norm that held true for most men. Agamemnon has just upbraided Diomedes and Sthenelos for being worse than their fathers. Sthenelos retorts:

> Son of Atreus, do not lie when you know how to speak truthfully. We boast to be far braver than our fathers. We two even took the seat of seven-gated Thebes, leading a

> smaller host against a stronger wall, in obedience to the
> signs of the gods and with the aid of Zeus. [Our fathers]
> were destroyed by their own boldness. Therefore, never
> place our fathers in honor equal to ours (404–10).

Since the sons succeeded where their fathers failed, Sthenelos judges his father's accomplishments realistically and will not abide the suggestion of his own inferiority. But what of the son who is unable to see his father for what he is, who regards his father's deeds as ever superior to his own, no matter how much less the father has achieved? Sophocles discovers such a mentality in Ajax, son of Telamon. Ajax cannot satisfy his desire to be like his father, and his culture has no signals to indicate that he has reached or exceeded his goal. Demands that are creative for most men become lethal for Ajax and lead to his disgrace and suicide.

On the day before the events that begin Sophocles' play, the army had voted to award the weapons of the dead Achilles to Odysseus. Deprived of his last opportunity to prove his *aretē*, Ajax goes mad. He leaves his hut during the night bent on slaying all the Greeks. Athena throws "notions hard to resist upon his eyes" (51), and he maims and kills animals instead. She affects his vision at the generals' camp after he has left his hut "burdened with anger over Achilles' arms" (41) and while he was already "pacing with mad sicknesses" (59). Calchas later attributes Athena's wrath to Ajax's prideful self-sufficiency in rejecting her support (749–80). Achilles and Diomedes, the foremost exemplars of the *aretē* standard, welcome divine aid, but Ajax goes unattended by a god throughout the battles at Troy. He is the protecting shield, the courageous lion (*Iliad* 11.548–57) with the stubbornness of the ass (11.558–65), whose foundations rest, as he himself boasts, upon his rearing:

No one will drive me back by his will against mine through force or skill, since I expect that I was not born or reared in Salamis so unskilled (7.197–99).

The goddess vents her resentment in a night and a day; Ajax's madness reaches back in time for its causes to his youth in Salamis.

Agamemnon encourages Teucer "to raise Telamon in honor," for Telamon had nurtured him in his house although Teucer was a bastard (8.281–85). How much more strongly would that burden be felt by the son born of Telamon's wife, the heir to his household, since Agamemnon can speak with understanding of the importance of Telamon's rearing for his sons? Sophocles transposes that element of background into "the psychological strain on Ajax of having a hero of a previous Trojan campaign for his father" [Stanford, 1963, p. xiii].

In their first ode after entering, the Salaminian sailors of the chorus sing of Ajax with knowledge that outstrips their conscious awareness:

Better that man who is sick and useless hide in Hades. Although he comes from his father's stock foremost among toiling Achaeans, no longer abiding by the character inbred through his rearing, he stays apart. Poor father, what unendurable ruin of your son awaits for you to hear, a ruin such as no lifetime of Aeacus' sons has nurtured before him (635–45).

The sailors do not wish that Ajax were dead; their safety depends upon his life. They seek to describe a madman, someone beside himself and far removed from the character instilled by his paternal rearing. They do not imagine that Ajax's downfall derives from the nurture he received over the years. Their last words should mean no more than that Ajax's disaster is unlike any that has befallen

Telamon's household. But the language exceeds the ordinary to betray a link between ruin and rearing. R.P. Winnington-Ingram concludes after a careful reading of this ode:

> if the words mean what they seem to say, then the poet is suggesting, through the subtleties of his lyric diction, that the *nosos* [sickness], which was the *atē* [ruin] of Ajax, is a long-continuing, long-fostered disease, bound up (as the Chorus fail to see) with his *syntrophoi orgai* [character inbred through his rearing]; that it is something which has grown with Ajax during his life-span, something that his life has bred [p. 38].

The source of Ajax's madness is inherent in the *aretē* standard itself. In wanting Achilles' weapons to prove his *aretē*, Ajax acts like any warrior. He defines his identity in terms of how much others approve of him. For Ajax, however, approval must come not from his peers but from his father or, more properly, the father he imagines. An ancient scholar remarking on line 434 recognizes: "He takes his father's successes passionately." During Heracles' expedition against Troy, after the walls of Troy were breached, Telamon entered the city before Heracles. The latter, enraged that another should usurp his glory, moved to slay Telamon. Realizing his peril, Telamon began gathering rocks. When the puzzled Heracles inquired the reason, Telamon responded that he was constructing an altar to "Heracles of the Beautiful Victory." In gratitude, Heracles awarded Telamon with Hesione, daughter of the king of Troy (Apollodorus, *Library* 2.6.4). The Ajax of the *Iliad* cannot understand why Achilles so prizes "a single woman" when he is being offered "seven best by far" (9.637–38). The Sophoclean Ajax, on the other hand, glorifies his father's prize with a hyperbole that characterizes the woman, even though Hesione is not his mother but

Teucer's, as "the most lovely part of the booty" and a "mighty garland of glory" (435; 465). He nowhere mentions Telamon's warlike feat of being the first to enter Troy. Ajax does not focus upon his father's accomplishments as a warrior; instead, he privileges the prize that his father receives. By the time of Achilles' death, he has fulfilled the expectations of a son, having far surpassed his father. But it is evident that Ajax esteems Telamon's glory beyond proportion and without regard for what he actually accomplished. In the place of a real father to rival, Ajax has fabricated an idealized father that has no meaning outside of his own desires.

Ajax lives by the social values of Homeric society. He believes that the son should imitate the father. Sitting on the ground, covered with the blood of the butchered animals that lie about him, he asks that his child Eurysaces be brought to him:

> Lift him up, lift him here. He will not be afraid of seeing this newly slaughtered gore if he is truly mine in what he has from his father. He must immediately be broken like a colt in the savage ways of his father and be made like him in nature. O son, be more fortunate than your father, but in all else be like him (545–51).

As long as Eurysaces remains ignorant of joy and pain, he remains his "mother's delight" (559), but when he reaches awareness, Ajax insists: "you must see to it that you will show what sort you are, from what sort of father you were nurtured, amid his enemies" (556–57). Ajax came to Troy for that same purpose, and he anticipated leaving, like his father, laden with glory:

> My father from the Trojan land won the most lovely part of the booty and came home bearing every glory. I, his son, to this same Troyland having come with no lesser

strength and having performed no smaller deeds of hand,
I perish thus dishonored among Argives (434–40).

Ajax has looked to his father, apparently from youth, to
define what sort of man he himself is, and his desire for
the arms of Achilles is induced by his compulsion to imitate
what his father has achieved. René Girard's concept of
mimetic desire illuminates Ajax's experience:

> In all the varieties of desire examined by us, we have en-
> countered not only a subject and an object but a third
> presence as well: the rival. It is the rival who should be
> accorded the dominant role. . . . The rival desires the same
> object as the subject, and to assert the primacy of the rival
> can lead to only one conclusion. Rivalry does not arise
> because of a fortuitous convergence of two desires on a
> single object; rather, *the subject desires the object because the
> rival desires it.* In desiring an object the rival alerts the sub-
> ject to the desirability of the object. The rival, then, serves
> as a model for the subject, not only in regard to such sec-
> ondary matters as style and opinions but also, and more
> essentially, in regard to desires [1977, p. 145].

In Girard's terms, the subject is Ajax, and the object is
Achilles' weapons. The rival is not Telamon the man himself but Telamon the idealized father. Ajax, competing
against a rival of his own imagining, wants the weapons
to prove that he has surpassed his father's glory. His desire
for the weapons springs from what he believes his father
would want and get. When he does not obtain "every
glory" and therefore cannot imitate his father, Ajax pictures himself naked before him:

> What sort of eye shall I show my father Telamon when I
> appear? How shall he endure to look upon me, appearing
> naked, without prizes of valor, for which he himself had
> a mighty garland of glory (462–65)?

More is implied in the image of nakedness than "without armour and arms" [Stanford, 1963, p. 118]. Ajax pictures himself a newborn child; without the weapons, he has not merely lost face (*omma*, literally, eye); he has lost his very being and the Telamonian nature which he must somehow prove to his father:

> Some attempt must be sought whereby I shall show the old man, my father, that I was not born from him gutless in nature (470–72).

Homeric society, as we have seen, and its counterpart in the aristocratic ethic of Sophocles' Athens were founded upon competition. As a man strove to be first among men, he also strove to be better and more famous than his father. Such is Hector's wish for his son Astyanax: "Someone might say of him, 'He is better by far than his father' " (*Iliad* 6.479). The son, to prove his paternal legacy, had to leave his father and father's household and risk his life in war. Achilles and Ajax come to Troy, while Hector, who will soon afterwards isolate himself from his father (*Iliad* 22.77–78), imagines his son "coming up [to the city] from the fighting" (*Iliad* 6.480). Yet the son must also survive the fighting to inherit his father's property and possessions and to pass them on to his son, thereby elaborating a twofold imperative that is the dilemma embedded in the *aretē* standard.

Ajax strives to be better than Telamon, but he rivals not his real father but a father idealized beyond all reality. Sophocles makes this point by the stark contrast between Telamon's command, "Be strong always with god" (765), and Ajax's rebuff, "Father, any man, a nothing, could possess power with the gods. I am sure I will get this glory even apart from them" (767–69). The source of Ajax's imbalance—what is wrong with him and what others perceive as pride—is his desire to exceed Telamon's glory as it never was. "Telamonian Ajax," like Peleus' son Achilles, expresses the tension between *daimon* (destiny), defined by past members of the family, and *ēthos* (individual character). When Achilles acts in accord with the nature and social role laid down by his father, Homer refers to him as Peleides and Aeacides, that is, the son of his father Peleus or of his grandfather Aeacus. When he fails to follow his father's advice, he is simply Achilles [Benardete, p. 12]. Most characteristic of Achilles is his wrath; most striking in Ajax is his desire to be *Telamonios*, to be "like (*-ios*) Telamon." Apart from that drive, one esteemed by his culture, Ajax is without being until he discovers his identity and the measure of his humanity in his woeful cries of *aiai* (430, 432).* Homer depicts the father as the source of continuity and order. Sophocles' very Homeric *Ajax* discovers in the father the focus of a flaw in the cultural fabric, namely, the lack of restraints on the son's drive to surpass his father. Ajax conforms to his society's standards too strictly and gets trapped by their failings. He finds release alone on the shore, even as he would pass his society's failings on to his son.

*The usual practice of using Ajax for the Greek Aias conceals the meaning of these cries. Ajax hears his destiny in the wailing of suffering.

Four

The Ideology of Sacrifice in Mythmaking

Rituals are formal actions performed according to rules and customs validated by the passage of time. Primarily social actions, they define the identity of the participating group as an entity distinct from all others, while within the group they demarcate the relative status among members. For the Greeks, rituals encouraged the fertility of fields, domestic animals, and women; they appeased an angry god or daimon; they brought about the sacrifice of an animal victim; they effected passage from one status to another. Today, rituals are most commonly associated with religion and, above all, with rites performed by someone specially trained and ordained, officiating before a congregation in a building consecrated for the purpose.

Rituals may be religious without being associated with a divinity. Plutarch in the *Moralia* describes the following ceremony which took place in his native city of Chaeronea in Boeotia:

> There is a traditional rite which the magistrate does in the common hearth, and each of the others does in his household. It is called the "Driving Out Bad Famine." Striking one of the house slaves with branches of willow, they drive him out through the doors, shouting after him, "Out with Bad Famine. In with Wealth and Health." When I was magistrate, many men took part in the rite. When we did

the customary things and had sat down again, there arose
an inquiry, first, about the name itself, then, about the
words shouted at the man being pursued, and, most of
all, about the incident and its circumstances (693e–94a).

This rite promotes the fertility of the city and its households by driving out a slave who takes famine with him.
The slave belongs to the group closely enough for its evil
forces to be attached to him but not as closely as a citizen
or kinsman, whose expulsion, in provoking retribution,
would be harmful. Lest those forces contaminate something fruitful, the slave is beaten with branches of a tree
thought to induce sterility and the loss of sexual desire.
The slave was probably driven from the family hearth, the
fireplace where its food was cooked and the rites to secure
its safety, fertility, and abundance were performed. By the
magic of agrarian rituals, Wealth and Health, made real
like Hesiod's Plenty and Poverty (*Theogony*, 593), are induced through the visible expulsion of the slave to enter
the house and city. The rite is religious in that it seeks to
sway the *mysterium* that is the earth, but no god is invoked,
and no priest officiates. In the ensuing discussion, the
unity displayed in doing "the customary things" gives way
to the multiplicity of opinions concerning their meaning.
The incident illustrates the imperative of a cult: its rites
must be performed in the traditional manner—the existence of the community or household depends upon it—
but no dogma or required beliefs are imposed upon the
worshippers regarding the significance of actions themselves.

The English word "religion" is misleading in speaking
about Greek practices. In so far as "religion" connotes a
received doctrine and some form of clerical hierarchy, it
carries with it the polarities of religious/secular, public/
personal, orthodox/heterodox, church/state—dichotomies
unknown to the religious life of the Greek. Greek priests

derived their authority to perform specific rites from the city or inherited them as a family obligation. Soothsayers, interpreters of omens, and oracles of the gods, particularly Zeus and Apollo, were recognized as having expertise in religious matters, but their pronouncements were never binding. *Eusebeia* (piety), which refers to any action that shows proper awe for what ought to be revered, is as close as the Greek language comes to a word for religion. Objects of reverence include not only the gods but one's parents, kinsmen, and fellow citizens, burial of the dead, and adherence to oaths. A young Athenian upon attaining his maturity swore allegiance to the state in the shrine of Aglauros. Any offense he might subsequently commit against the state would break his oath and become an offense against the gods and against *eusebeia*. Never a matter of personal or private convictions but of public and social bonds, *eusebeia* is tantamount to loyalty to gods, family, and *polis*.

So deeply did religion infuse the existence of the Greeks that to single out one quality that denoted the pious was impossible for the ordinary man. In Plato's dialogue *Euthyphro*, Socrates asks Euthyphro, who professes to know the holy, what holiness is. Euthyphro cannot tell him; he can only give instances of holy acts. The pious man revered those things and acts that made life possible and preserved the *polis*, things which remained above the personal beliefs of the individual and beyond any doubt.

In performing their rites, Greeks were concerned less with the personality of the gods than with the gods' ability to aid or protect them. They generally referred to them simply as "the god" or "the gods" without the specificity found in myths. In their cults, the Greeks denoted the god in a particular manifestation of his power by the use of an adjective. Zeus was worshipped as Zeus Horios when he was responsible for preserving boundary stones, as Zeus Epakrios for sending the rain, as Zeus Teleios for overseeing marriage, and as Zeus Polieus for protecting the city. None of these Zeuses bears an obvious resemblance to the Zeus of Homer, father of gods and men, but the grounds for these manifestations are present in the Homeric Zeus's concern for guests and hosts and for justice. Still, anthropomorphism, the making of gods in human shape, was an activity of poets. Gods, despite being integral to Greek religious mentality, are hopelessly at odds among themselves. The chastity demanded by Artemis drew upon her devotee, Hippolytus, the wrath of Aphrodite, goddess of sexual passion. Confusion of the gods of myths created by the poets thwarts Euthyphro's attempt to define the holy as that which the gods love, since what one god loves another hates. To the extent that mythmaking touched religion, it provided those who would ponder the nature of deity and divine justice with material for reflection in forming theology and philosophy.

More often, rituals were used to interpret myths that had themselves nothing to do with rituals. The mythmaker tells his story as if looking through a glass made of rituals. The rites of sacrificing cattle, sheep, pigs, or goats to an Olympian deity lie behind much mythmaking, especially on the tragic stage in Athens. One reason, no doubt, is the centrality of the ritual to Greek cults. Another is the resemblance of slaughtering an animal to murdering a human being. A large animal's throat was pierced and its blood made to spurt onto the altar. The practice, gruesome in physical reality, seems incongruous with the metaphysical role attributed to it by religious belief.

In *thusia* (blood sacrifice), the participants form a procession to conduct the victim to the altar of the god. The altar is raised from the ground and stained with the blood of countless victims. Nearby stands a bowl ready to receive the blood of yet another. The participants are wearing garlands; they have bathed and donned clean clothes, signs of their freedom from the pollution of homicide. One brings the lustral, or ceremonial, water. The victim's head is garlanded; its horns have been gilded with gold. At the front of the procession, a virgin carries on her head a basket in which a knife is hidden beneath coarse barley grains. The procession moves rhythmically to singing and the sounds of a flute. The victim walks without hesitation or prodding [Stengl; Rudhardt, pp. 257–66; Burkert, 1966, pp. 104–13; 1983, pp. 3–12].

Once at the altar, the procession, led by the virgin, circles the altar to the right. The participants wash their hands and sprinkle the victim's head with water. They wait for it to shake its head, and, if necessary, repeat the procedure until it complies. They wet its head a second time or until it bows. The participants take the barley grains from the basket. After a brief moment of silence and a spoken prayer, they hurl the barley at the victim, the altar, and the earth. Removing the knife from the basket, the chief sacrificer cuts hairs from the victim's head and throws them into the fire. Then he plunges the point of the knife into the victim's throat. Women scream out shrilly, "ololu, ololu, ololu. . . . " The blood shoots out, not to be allowed to fall directly to the ground. Small victims are lifted over the altar; larger ones, incapacitated by the stroke of an axe, have their necks drawn back so the spurting blood may hit the altar, or the blood is caught in the bowl and poured over the altar. The thigh bones and small pieces of meat, the god's portion, are removed and burned with incense upon the altar. The internal organs most suffused with blood and so most numinous—heart, lungs, liver, and kidneys—are roasted without salt and eaten immediately. Afterwards, the participants throw wine and cakes into the fire. The fire dies down, and the rite is complete. Those parts of the meat specified by tradition are given to the chief sacrificer. The rest is stewed with vegetables and spices for the feast that culminates most Greek festivals. The victim's hide goes to the sanctuary or temple to be sold off for support and revenue to buy new victims, while the skull is thrown upon the pile with those of the past, visible evidence of the worshippers' piety. How quickly the fearful confrontation with the deity descends to the banalities of men's earthly existence!

Religious man, in Walter Burkert's description [1983, p. 3], is *homo necans*, "killing man," he who approaches the deity through blood. To sacrifice means slaughtering a victim and consuming its blood-rich innards. The common view considered sacrifice a bestowing of gifts upon the god with the understanding that the god would reciprocate with a benefit. The rites themselves present another picture; they seem preoccupied with the relationship between man and victim and governed by a twofold imperative: the victim must consent to the taking of its blood, while the sacrificers must appear innocent of its slaughter. Homicides are taboo because their pollution would contaminate the ritual, turning it into murder.

The ritual starts with the procession which sends the victim to the altar. The sounds of singing and flute playing contrast with the silence just before immolation. Through the procession the participants withdraw from the profane. Walking toward the altar, they leave behind everyday time and space and draw near the sacred. As the procession moves around the altar, it is marked off from its environs. Here, the separate spheres of gods and men overlap as the divine impinges upon the human. As Edmund Leach observes [p. 82], the altar becomes a bridge that joins the human with the divine realm, so that the victim's blood is shed not in the territory of the community but at a point belonging completely to neither the sacred nor profane.

The victim is a domesticated animal. Bulls, cows, sheep, goats, and pigs were used. The fact that the animals could not exist in the same form apart from human tending creates a semblance between donors and victim. Domestication enables the animal to stand in and be substituted for the donors, creating a channel between human and divine by animal, not human blood. The garlands worn by men and animal symbolize this relationship. Wild animals, creatures of the savage and separate from the civilized realms of farm and city, could not be offered. Between such animals and men no agreements were possible; they were for hunting and killing. Similarly, resistance or balking by the victim would destroy the identification. Much anxiety must have been felt over upsetting the animal.

The rites at the altar begin with water. The participants wash their hands, a cleansing act that signifies their unity. They wet the victim's head to obtain its consent; they will not proceed until they do so, since, otherwise, its death would be murder. The animal shakes its head to get rid of the water, but *homo necans* deceives himself into believing what he needs to believe. Once the victim consents by shaking and bowing its head, the participants pelt its body with barley. This initial act of violence unites them in a common aggression against the victim. A second act, the clipping of the hairs, assaults the victim more directly, rendering it no longer inviolate. At the moment when it falls beneath the fatal stroke, women cry out. Their shrieks, punctuating the violence, salute and recognize in spontaneous emotion the mingled joy and terror at the god's advent as the blood streams forth from the severed throat onto the altar. By drawing the neck back upward in the direction of the Olympian gods, the sacrificer consecrates the blood and summons the god's power. As so many times before, the altar runs with blood, soaked with a substance too numinous to let it fall to the earth. Blood must be kept from polluting the community by channeling it across the altar.

The fire blazing on the altar transforms the offerings. It consumes the shorn hairs entirely. Their scent ascends in smoke along the route soon to be taken by the savor of the burned thigh pieces and bones. The god, delighting in the aroma of the meat intertwined with the scent of incense, may, in return, bestow his power and attention upon the sacrificers. The humans partake of the divine presence in the victim by roasting the quivering organs on spits and eating them, for these parts are too filled with divine potency to be taken away from the altar. Those who taste them are bound by the strongest ties. The meat, which is not considered sacred, is shared among others, even on occasion with someone not present at the sacrifice.

The rites of *thusia* impart meaning to objects and acts of the ordinary world, not themselves intrinsically meaningful, by investing them with the power to move the worshippers from the everyday toward the unearthly and atemporal. Through the ritual slaughter of a bull or sheep, the participants admit their mortality, for mortals alone sacrifice and eat cooked meat.

We have already seen in Hesiod's myth of Prometheus how sacrifice removes the males of Mekone from a state of paradise and how the analogous activities, marriage and agriculture, complete their acculturation. Hesiod reproduces a mythic tradition that views sacrifice as a fall from a better time when men were free of war and the slaughter of victims. "All things were gentle and kindly to men," the philosopher and mystic Empedocles (c. 493–c. 433) of Akragas in Sicily recites in his *Purifications*, "beasts and birds and friendliness spread abroad" (fr. 130). Men knew only Aphrodite, whom they propitiated with statues and paintings, offerings of myrrh and frankincense, and libations of honey. The contradiction between physical reality and metaphysical belief comes out strongly in Empedocles' lament in the *Purifications*:

> The altar was not soaked with the pure murder of bulls, but the greatest abomination among men was to tear out their life and eat the goodly limbs (fr. 128).

The rites themselves, however, correspond to an opposing myth of the origin of civilization. Instead of by a fall from near divinity, civilization comes into being by ascension from primordial bestiality. In one version, that of the third-century tragedian Moschion, men at first live in caves and kill one another for food:

> There was once that age when humans had a mode of life like the beasts and dwelled in mountain caves and sunless ravines. For there was not yet the roofed house or wide city fortified by stone towers. The black glebe, nurse of grain, was not cut by curved plows, nor was the worker, the iron pruning hook, tending to the flourishing gardens of Bacchus' wine. But the earth was barren, holding silent, and flowing with water. Food of eaten flesh gave [humans] a way of life spent in killing one another. The law was humble, and violence sat on the throne beside Zeus. The weak were the food of the stronger. When time which produces and nourishes all things changed human life again, either by bringing forth the care of Prometheus or by necessity or by providing through long practice nature herself as teacher, then the fruit of pure Demeter's cultivated nourishment and the sweet stream of Bacchus were discovered. The earth, before unseeded, was plowed by yoked oxen. Men girded cities with towers and constructed roofed houses and converted their savage ways to civilized life. From then on, law laid it down to cover the dead in tombs and to portion earth for unburied dead and not to leave them in sight as a memorial of their former feasts (fr. 6).

Both traditions reverse the reality of Greeks building houses, practicing agriculture, and burying their dead. Their differences cannot be resolved, however, because mythmakers extrapolate in diametrically opposed directions. They imagine a superior situation, such as Hesiod's males of Mekone, or an inferior one like Moschion's murderous cannibals.

Sacrifice puts an end to cannibalism by providing humans with a better source of food. The cook in Athenion's *Samothracians*, a third-century comedy, prides himself as a culture hero because of his skill:

> That art has freed us from a bestial and lawless life. From disgusting cannibalism it has led us to order and the life we now live. At a time when cannibalism and all sorts of evils existed, a man arose who was no simpleton, the first to sacrifice a victim and roast the meat. And since the meat was nicer than human flesh, they no longer chewed one another, but sacrificed and roasted sheep. And once they had experienced that pleasure, with the beginning behind them, they advanced the cook's art further. But mindful of that day of earlier customs, they roast in the flame the innards in honor of the gods without adding salt, for they had not yet discovered its use. . . . What alone proved to be the salvation of us all were our zeal in adding to our skill and the use of sauces and seasonings, which advanced still further the cook's art. . . . Then someone introduced the stuffed paunch, cooked a kid so that it melted in your mouth, gave it distinction with fine trimmings, a gentle touch of grape-syrup, a bit of fish smuggled in, some greens, rich smoked fish, groats, and honey. Because of these delights, everyone kept aloof from eating a man's corpse. Everyone consented to live with one another, a populace came together, cities were civilized, all through the art of cookery (fr. 1).

The cook's hyperbolic praise reflects the role of cooking in *thusia* itself. Cooking, as Marcel Detienne has shown, constitutes a metaphor for the evolution of human culture [1979, pp. 75–79]. Roasting the viscera on spits occurs between the throwing of unmilled barley and the boiling of meat in a cauldron. The barley remains in its raw or natural state. Roasting applies the techniques of culture to singe the outside while leaving the inside rare or even raw. Boiling thoroughly cooks the meat. The roasted innards are eaten without salt, salt being an accoutrement of culture;

the meat is prepared with condiments and vegetables as a stew. The succession from raw to roasting to boiling retraces the evolution of humanity from savagery to civilization. The transitions from raw grains to milled flour baked into cakes and from water to wine are redundant expressions of this evolution. Sacrifice, then, also affirms the condition of the participants as civilized human beings and their status as citizens of a *polis*.

The rites of the festival of the Ox-Murder (Bouphonia) and their related myths put the dynamics of sacrificial ideology into question [Parke, pp. 162–67; Vernant, 1981; Burkert, 1983, pp. 136–43]. On the fourteenth day of Skirophorion (June), in the god's precinct on the Acropolis, the Athenians celebrated the Bouphonia during the festival of Zeus Polieus (Zeus in his capacity as protector of the city). The use of the double axe and of a bronze table instead of an altar suggests a Mycenaean origin for the ritual, since these implements were prominent during the period. The claim by the geographer Pausanias (second century A.D.) that the murder of the ox first took place in the time of King Erechtheus implies an early date for the ritual. By the fifth century, the Bouphonia had become an oddity, but its rites continued to be practiced at least into the second century A.D. Barley and wheat or meal in honeyed oil were placed unguarded upon a table, and selected oxen were driven past it. Whichever animal touched the holy things was struck with the axe and skinned with the knife. The slayer, a cult functionary called the Ox-Murderer or Ox-Smiter, dropped the axe and fled. The axe and knife were then brought to trial, condemned, and cast out of the community; the knife and probably the axe were thrown into the sea. The ox's hide was stuffed with hay and set in front of a plow. Although the festival was little understood and likely attended only by those whose duty it was to perform the ceremony, that the rites belonged to the festival of Zeus Polieus indicates their importance.

The most extensive source for the rituals of the Bouphonia is from a work by Porphyry (A.D. 232/33–c. 305), *On Abstaining from Living Things*, in which Porphyry advocates vegetarianism.

Diomos, a priest of Zeus Polieus, first slaughtered the ox because, during the festival of Zeus Polieus when the grain was prepared in the age-old manner, the ox approached and tasted the sacred meal. Taking the rest who were present as helpers, he slew it (2.10).

. . . .

At a public sacrifice in Athens, after the meal in honeyed oil and incense were set out on the table in plain sight, ready to be sacrificed to the gods, one of the oxen coming in from the fields is said to have eaten some of the meal and to have trampled on the rest. A certain Diomos or Sopatros, not a native but someone farming in Attica, became enraged at what had happened. He seized an axe that was being sharpened nearby and struck the ox. The ox died. When the man recovered from his anger and realized what he had done, he buried the ox and went of his own accord into exile in Crete as one who had committed impiety. Then the rain stopped falling, and the grain no longer grew. Delegates were sent by the state to Delphi to inquire of Apollo. The priestess of Apollo responded:

> the exile in Crete will redeem these [drought and barrenness], and vengeance having been taken on the murderer and the dead having been resurrected in the same sacrifice in which [the dead] died, those who taste the dead and do not hold back will be better off.

A search was undertaken, and the man responsible for the deed was located. Sopatros reckoned that he would be released from the unpleasantness of being polluted if they all did these measures in common. He told those who came to him that the ox must be slain by the city. Since they were at their wits' end over who would be the slayer, he offered them this possibility: if they enrolled him as a citizen, they would share the murder with him. Agreement was reached on those terms. When they came back to the city, they arranged the affair in the way in which it remains today.

They chose girls to bring the water. They fetched the water used for sharpening the axe and the knife. After the sharpening, one man delivered the axe, another struck the ox, and a third thrust the point of the knife into the throat. They skinned it, and everyone tasted the ox. Afterwards, having sewn up the hide of the ox and stuffed it with hay, they set it to the plow as if ready for work. Assembling a trial for murder, they summoned everyone who had participated in the deed to defend himself. The water-fetchers charged that the sharpeners were more to blame than they. The sharpeners said the same about the axe-deliverer, and this one of the throat-cutter, and this one of the knife which, being without a voice, was condemned for murder. . . . They threw the knife into the sea (2.29–30).

The ritual of the Bouphonia depends upon the heightened metonymy between the bestial and the human that characterizes the plow ox. It is no ordinary animal that is slain but one that has returned from the fields where it has labored beside men to provide them with food. In Athens, it was a criminal offense to slay a plow ox. From its contact with men, the plow ox becomes "too human" and thus unsuitable for sacrifice, for human beings cannot be eaten—an essential aspect of *thusia*. Since sacrificing a plow ox virtually entails cannibalism, thereby undoing the acculturation achieved by the progress of time, its immolation provides a test of the ritual and of the logic of blood sacrifice; that is, if the sacrifice of a victim so close to men is not murder, then the sacrifice of other domesticated animals cannot be murder.

The myth accompanying Porphyry's description of the Bouphonia places the murder of the ox at a time before blood sacrifice, when only cakes and grain were offered to the gods. The myth belongs to the tradition that pictures sacrifice as terminating men's innocence of bloodshed and as distancing them from the gods. We need not ask whether an age of bloodless offerings existed. The question derives from our sense of historical process and of the effect of time on conditioning ways of thought and social circumstances, which the Greeks had not yet developed. From a modern historical viewpoint, the question calls for evidence outside the myths. The Greeks postulated this bloodless period on different evidence, the rituals of blood sacrifice. For them, the matter was not one of history but of attitudes toward sacrifice. As a historical phenomenon, sacrifice may have arisen out of hunters' rituals to restore the victim's life in some fashion and to allay their repulsion over the act of killing. In any event, after the introduction of agriculture, the practice was kept alive, perhaps out of fear of discontinuing it or for its ability to strengthen group identity, but domestic animals replaced the scarce wild ones. Whatever the origin may be, anxiety and guilt attend the rites, as is apparent from the twofold imperative of *thusia*; from Sopatros' pollution and exile in Porphyry's myth; from the accusations and counteraccusations of the participants in the ritual; and from the condemnation and expulsion of the axe and knife. Both myth and ritual seek to assure the sacrificer that these emotions are groundless.

Porphyry's myth explains sacrifice by strategies that divert responsibility for its origin away from the community. Sopatros is a foreigner, an alien resident in Attica as a farmer. Moreover, he does not slay the ox deliberately but while deranged by anger. The ox is partly to blame for its death, for it desecrated holy things. The axe seems to be put at fault for being handy. The murder of the ox and the ensuing sacrifice are thus represented as having been inflicted upon the community by outsiders. Athenians are not to blame.

More than other animals, the plow ox confuses the differences between the human and the bestial. Its slaying becomes murder, a term ordinarily applicable only to humans. Sopatros buries the ox as he would a man and, polluted with murder, goes into exile in Crete. Barrenness and drought oppress the land. As phenomena of the physical world, barrenness and drought bring about the community's demise by starvation and thirst; as religious signs, they reveal hidden contamination in the same way that the plague in Sophocles' *Oedipus the King* (c. 425) indicates the pollution caused by the presence in Thebes of Laius' murderers [Girard, 1974, pp. 833–45; 1977, pp. 76–77]. But as elements in a myth, barrenness and drought have no external referent, that is, they do not refer to a real barrenness or drought. They signify the loss of differences between the human and bestial created by Sopatros. They can do so because, like the plague in *Oedipus the King*, barrenness and drought kill indiscriminately, breaking down the "order of things" normal to human life. They may destroy young before old, strong before feeble, children before parents.

The oracle, in turn, reflects this loss of difference by directing the community to atone for the loss of the ox's life with that of a man. "Vengeance having been taken on the murderer" can have no other meaning than killing Sopatros. On the other hand, in context, "the dead having been resurrected in the same sacrifice in which [the dead] died" could refer to Sopatros or the ox. The subject of the verb translated as "died" is not stated and could be animal or human; both would be dead at this point. By one reading of the oracle, then, the community may avenge the murder of this quasi-human animal by slaying and eating a man. Yet an oracle "neither speaks out nor conceals but points" (Heraclitus, fr. 93). Sopatros atones for his deed and rids himself of pollution by another reading of the oracle: he substitutes an animal for himself; it dies and is eaten.

Sopatros acts like a sacrificer at a time when, as depicted by the myth, animals were not offered. Slaying the ox in such circumstances is murder, whether committed by Sopatros or someone else; that accounts for the community's consternation over who would be the slayer. But what is murder when done by the individual becomes sacrifice when done by the group. Sopatros joins the group and, by becoming a citizen, polarizes the community's violence against the ox as a common victim. All slay it. His strategy restores the difference between humans who wreak violence and animals who suffer it. No man is a murderer because all are murderers. The myth reveals that men avoid killing one another by uniting to kill animals in order to forestall killing one another. The sacrifice of the ox by Sopatros' reading of the oracle replaces the murder of a man ordained by the other reading of the oracle. But the myth does not suppress the other possible victim, Sopatros. The myth denies a murder took place by spreading responsibility for killing the ox among all members of the community. The ritual achieves the same result by directing the blame at member after member.

After the sacrifice and tasting of the meat, the community conducts a trial. The unity created through its violence against an animal is shattered as each participant accuses the other of the crime of murder. Sacrifice has disappeared in murder and, with it, the distinction between the ox as sacrificial victim and as murder victim as well as that between sacrificer and murderer. All participants are equally guilty, yet each would distinguish himself by erecting the difference innocent/guilty where no such difference is possible. There results an outburst of what René Girard calls "reciprocal violence," because it effects a vicious circle of reprisals that would destroy the community [1977, pp. 43–49]. Reciprocity ends; violence ceases to go back and forth among members and is focused again on a common victim when the difference between

voiced/voiceless is established. Unlike the other participants in the slaughter and eating of the ox, the knife cannot
speak. No more guilty than any other, it has no voice with
which to pass on the blame and to avoid becoming the
victim by substituting someone else. All condemn the knife
and cast it into the sea, ridding the community of the
pollution of murder. The knife, in a word, is scapegoated.

With opposing strategies, the myth and ritual of the
Bouphonia deny that the sacrifice of a plow ox is murder.
According to the myth, everyone took part; with no one
more guilty than the others, there is no one to charge with
murder. The ritual puts the blame upon the knife and the
axe, which are condemned for the crime and expelled from
the community. The ox is filled with its proper food and
put back to work. No murder has been committed since
the ox has been "resurrected."

Sacrificial ideology and the strategies that we have observed in the rituals of *thusia* and the Bouphonia inform
Sophocles' interpretation of the Ajax myth. The tragedian
and Porphyry share the same cultural understanding of
blood sacrifice. Their concepts of *thusia* reflect their common acculturation in Greek religious ritual. Thus, and despite the difference of medium and purpose, the work of
one may be used to illuminate that of the other.

In the rites of *thusia*, everyone takes part in the immolation of the victim, and all agree to deceive themselves
into denoting the act as piety. Their deception always succeeds because they are deceiving themselves. No one
stands outside the ritual to expose their deception. In *Ajax*,
Sophocles puts his audience into the position of being such
an observer. No matter how familiar those in the theater
are with sacrifice and the myth of Ajax, they cannot control
what happens on stage before them. Sophocles exposes
the sacrificer as a murderer through Ajax, who falls upon
animals in hostile attack.

Tragedy, as we have seen, imperils definitions of the

human condition. Time, which, in *thusia*, irreversibly traces movement toward a higher state of civilization, comes undone in Sophocles' *Ajax* by Ajax's slaughter of animals. Scholars are uncertain whether Sophocles took this from the tradition or created it himself. Nonetheless, to an audience for whom a "meat-working [butchering] day" (Aeschylus, *Agamemnon* 1592) connoted sacrifice, such slaughter would have evoked sacrifice, even if Sophocles had not used sacrificial language to describe Ajax's deed. Ostensibly, Sophocles dramatizes the disgrace and suicide of Ajax and the ensuing quarrel of the Greek leaders over his corpse. But the action of the play is determined at a less evident level by the patterns and strategies developed to conceal the irresolvable flaw in sacrifice, namely, its resemblance to murder. Sophocles poses the problem of sacrifice as one concerning Ajax, so that his audience may mistake the real problem and fall into the trap of pondering the wrong question. The play asks not "What kind of man is Ajax?" but "What kind of act is sacrifice?"

Ajax sets out during the night to slay the whole Greek force. An insane plan, it could hardly have succeeded. In any case, Athena diverts his aggression away from men onto animals. But in Ajax's eyes and mind, they are men. Ajax does not sacrifice them; he murders them, seeing and thinking them to be men. Their numinous blood is profaned, smeared over Ajax, his hut, and the Argive land.

Naked aggression against helpless animals is unthinkable in a sane man. Sopatros slays the ox while out of his mind with rage. The same motif explains the slaying of Artemis' tame bear in one of the foundation myths of her rites at Brauron; the bear is killed by a man enraged over its mutilation of his sister (Scholiast on Aristophanes, *Lysistrata* 645). The chorus of Salaminian sailors assumes that Ajax did not fall upon herds of flocks "from his own mind"

(182). It is "unthinkable," because to slaughter animals of the sort to be sacrificed undermines sacrifice itself and therefore civilization. This is the tacit assumption Sophocles' audience and the author share. Ajax could have accomplished no more than the murder of men in his mad attack upon the army. Instead, he undoes the power of ritualized killing of animals by exposing its function as a substitute for the internecine violence of man against man.

As the play opens, a man enters cautiously; he is scrutinizing the ground before him. He has already come within the wall enclosing the hut in the background. Athena, recognizable from her dress and armor, watches from above, looking down upon the man from atop the hut. The audience quickly learns that the man is Odysseus and that he is following Ajax's trail of mingled human and animal tracks. Odysseus walks erect between the goddess above him and the animal tracks below him. The scene visually represents Odysseus firmly situated in the midspace between divine and bestial that constitutes civilization. He stands in graphic contrast to Ajax, who, having descended to the bestial, has withdrawn from human space.

Called from his hut by Athena, Ajax appears before her, carrying a whip and red with the blood he believes to be human. Removed from the human by virtue of his savagery, Ajax is depicted, in a seeming paradox, as ascending toward the divine in that, unlike Odysseus, he sees Athena and shares with her an ethic that glories in the fall of an enemy. He regards the goddess as his "ally," deeming her, in the parlance of imperialistic Athens, a subordinate to whom he gives orders [Knox, 1961, pp. 8–9]. In reducing sacrifice to murder, Ajax has obliterated the differences between human and divine as well as between human and bestial that its rites affirm. The poles whose existence depends upon those differences collapse into one.

Tecmessa saw Ajax in the hut butchering and torturing animals; although ignorant of the meanings of his actions, she likens them to sacrifice:

> Such things you could see inside the hut, the victims slain by his hand, bathed in blood, that man's sacrificial victims full of portent (218–20);
> . . .
> He cut the throats of some on the ground inside (235);
> . . .
> Turning others upward, he cut their throats (298–99).

Ajax's tragedy begins when he hears from Tecmessa how he has come to be in a hut "full of disaster." "When he looked around the hut full of disaster, he struck his head and wailed; he was sitting, a ruin amid the ruins of the carcasses of his sheep murder" (307–9). Sophocles intensifies Tecmessa's report of Ajax's screams by cries of "O me" (333, 336) that come from within the hut, the first sounds uttered by the undeluded Ajax. Quickly, as if to shock the audience, the door of the hut opens, and Ajax, laid low among his victims, comes into view. He is wheeled out on a low platform (*ekkyklēma*) used to display interior scenes. His screams generate meaning by analogy with the women's shrieking in ritualistic sacrifice. Visually, the fallen Ajax is contrasted with the erect participants in sacrifice, and, aurally, his cries at the recognition that he has killed animals echo the ritualized cries at the death of the victim. The sacrificers remain in liminal space, while Ajax's descent to the bestial, prefigured by the trail into his hut, is reified by his appearance on the *ekkyklēma*. The women's screams culminate a common violence; Ajax's, his own mad attack. Their shrieks evince whatever emotions—horror, guilt, repulsion, awe—that the elaborate rites of blood sacrifice circumscribe. The women cry out in the presence of a god whose ever feared approach has been sought by prayers and by the immolation of a willing victim. Ajax "awakens" to find himself facing what he has perpetrated upon "fearless beasts" (366), the true terror of which derives from the primordial murder no longer confined and disguised by rituals. From madness and through clouded vision, naked and unprotected by the institutions of civilization, Ajax confronts the other forces, kept "other," outside civilization, by those same institutions [Segal, 1981, pp. 41–42]. His are the primal screams of a man in the presence of the savage and of the divine that humans call "god." Ajax withdraws into the hut; his wife and son remain outside. He has resolved to die.

When the audience next sees Ajax, he has risen from his carnage. He walks toward center stage; ignoring Tecmessa and his crew, he begins to speak: "All things unseen, vast time immensurable makes grow and hides when revealed" (646–47). He then announces what he plans to do: "I am going to the washing places and meadows by the sea so that by cleansing my defilements, I may escape the goddess' heavy wrath" (654–56). When he reappears in the next episode, the audience watches him fix Hector's sword in the ground and fall upon it. But Ajax does not simply kill himself. He sacrifices himself, the sword becoming his butcher-priest, his sacrificer-killer (815). Ajax goes to the meadows intent on sacrificing himself, and only Sophocles knew *in the second episode* that that would be the manner of his death *in the third episode* [Tyrrell, 1985, p. 166].

In the previous scene, Tecmessa describes for him the fate of his family left bereft of his protection. At the time her words have no effect, but during the intervening choral song they apparently influence him:

I, too, who used to do dreadful deeds of power then, as
by the dipping of iron, begin to be womanized in my *stoma*
by this woman. I pity leaving her widowed and my child
orphaned among enemies (650–53).

Out of pity for Tecmessa, Ajax suggests that his sword's
edge (*stoma*) has been softened, as has his mouth (*stoma*)
in voicing his pity. He plays on the two meanings of *stoma*
to mislead Tecmessa. Ajax is still determined to die, but
he so pities his woman and son that he will not declare
his intentions outright. The expression of his pity cuts two
ways: has he taken such pity for them that he will live, or
is he still determined to die (473–80) despite his pity? The
speech provides no inkling of the conclusion to be drawn.
Sophocles does not have him lie directly, since, as author,
he knows that Ajax of the second episode is more than
the sum of his roles as warrior, son, husband, and father.
He is a sacrificer, and as such cannot be made to lie, since
the sacrificer cannot lie about killing the victim. But he
does willfully deceive himself that its slaughter is not murder. That is what Ajax *homo necans* is doing. He is talking
about time, but, in terms of sacrificial ideology, the subject
of his speech is irrelevant as long as the speech is incon-
clusive. By speaking in language that affords more than
one reading, Ajax deceives others into believing that he is
not about to murder himself. Unlike the sacrificer, he deceives in order to substitute himself for a victim, and, unlike the victim, he does not need to be tricked in order to
go "voluntarily." Sacrificer and murderer, donor and victim, become one through words open to interpretation.

Ajax's speech comes at the point when a remedy for the
evils at hand would be sought from a god. The ox is dead,
enraging a god; a cure must be sought from Apollo. So it
is in the case of Sopatros, which rephrases without de-
coding the ideology. But Ajax prescribes his own cure; his
deception is analogous to the multivalent words of an or-

acle, which explains why Athena's revelation seems an afterthought. The angry goddess reveals the measures that would end her wrath against Ajax (753–57), but she is too late. The function of Athena's revelation has already been fulfilled by Ajax's speech. Pity and concern for his family account, in part only, for Ajax's deception. Deception is prompted as well by something outside the play—the complex of oracle and substitution.

The sword looms large in Sophocles' play because of its interference with the strategy of scapegoating. Ajax would hide it away, bury it in some trackless spot, but the sword cannot be banished. Neither is it innocent. Its complicity with Ajax in slaughtering the animals is underlined by the imagery of light and dark. The sword is, at first, a "gleaming iron" (147), "blazing ruin to the heavens" (195); later, Ajax becomes himself the "gleaming man" (221) who slays with "dark swords" (231). Positioned like the knife in the Bouphonia between the slaying of animals and the threatened slaying of a man, the sword does not protect Ajax by assuming the blame. It is made by Sophocles to negate the strategy of scapegoating in that nothing unique, nothing different, may be said of it without its opposite also being true. The sword is the "gift of Hector, most hated and hostile of [Ajax's] guest-friends" (817–18). It is a "no-gift gift" (665), for Ajax considers that he is being slain by Hector's sword (817–18). It belongs simultaneously to both men and to neither. The sword, like the knife in the Bouphonia, is personified as "murderer/sacrificer," whose "very kind" nature (822) is doubled as friend in ending Ajax's shame and as enemy in ending his life. It is no ordinary weapon, and Ajax is no ordinary man. And he dies no ordinary death.

Here, Sophocles takes advantage of his audience's familiarity with Ajax's cult in Athens and Salamis. The warrior's ability to defend his family terminated with his death. Ajax confounds life and death. Sophocles trans-

forms Ajax's corpse into something equivalent to the hero's tomb, so that his son Eurysaces and Tecmessa gain
from the dead Ajax the protection denied them by the
living. The scene evokes the tableau of the ox in the Bouphonia stuffed with hay and set again at the plow; in both
"resurrections," the dead defend the living.

For most readers, Sophocles' play loses its drama after
Ajax's death. The hero dies, to be replaced on stage by
lesser men who lack the fascination aroused by Ajax's brutal force. They wrangle and dispute over his corpse about
things that appear to have nothing to do with Ajax. The
fact is, they have nothing to do with him. Ajax is dead,
but in the final episode and *exodos*, Sophocles shows a
community stripped of its rituals and on the brink of de-
scending into the savagery of the mutilated corpse (1062–
65). The unburied Ajax confuses corpse with carrion, dead
with living, and lower world with upper world. From his
corpse, the violent effacement of differences brought about
by the "night Ajax" (217) radiates outward to become the
reciprocal violence of the final scenes.

These scenes reproduce the cascading accusations of the
Bouphonia in the absence of a Sopatros or a knife to channel the violence away from men. The wrangling of Agamemnon, Menelaus, and Teucer threatens verbally, as
Ajax's attack did physically, to sweep away the oppositions that define civilization. The first distinction to be lost
is that between Argive and Phrygian (that is, between
Greek and barbarian, friend and enemy): "We expected to
bring [Ajax] from home as an ally and friend, and we found
him more hostile than the Phrygians" (1052–54). In the
ensuing violence, distinctions between ruler and ruled
(1067–68;1103–4), noble and commoner (1093–96), bow and
shield (1120–23), foreign and personal enemy (1132–33),
are swept away.

Agamemnon enters, enraged at the affront to his sovereignty. He is already gripped by the oscillating violence

of charge and countercharge that held his brother and Teucer. W.B. Stanford's observation that "as usual one of the Atreidae acts as if he were identical with the other" [1963, p. 211] assumes added meaning when we realize it refers to a scene made of lost identities. That confusion is further heightened by the probability that the same actor played both brothers [Pavlovskis, pp. 116–17]. Agamemnon utters a truism: "Men of good understanding prevail everywhere" (1252); and a threat: "The great, broad ox nevertheless goes straight down the road at the urging of a little goad. I see this remedy coming your way soon unless you get some sense" (1253–56). He accuses Teucer of outrage: "You are acting outrageously, boldly, and running free at the mouth. Won't you learn moderation?" (1258–59). The leader of the chorus gives guidance for the scene: "O, that there would be the sense in both of you to learn moderation" (1264). Anger belies any claim to moderation, and the process of effacement continues: noble birth cannot be distinguished from slave birth (1228–30; 1299–1302), nor foreigner from native Greek (1262–63; 1291–92; 1295).

Teucer, Menelaus, and Agamemnon have each tried to assert something unique about himself or something different about his antagonist. They fail, but in the attempt they have been destroying the categories and polarities that structure their society. On the other hand, Agamemnon's and Menelaus' wrath far exceeds what the events seem to justify. They react with the primordial violence characterizing the age before sacrifice, the time of Moschion's murderers. What resulted from strife of this sort in a real situation may be found in Thucydides' description (3.82–83) of the revolt of the Corcyreans from Athenian rule during the Peloponnesian War: "They changed the usual meanings of words with a view toward their actions, claiming it their right" (3.82). Tragedy imitates violence, and Sophocles has already prepared his ending.

During the prologue, Sophocles locates Odysseus outside the violence kindled by Ajax's slaughter of beasts: "I see that we who live are nothing but phantoms and empty shadows" (125–26). Now, Sophocles elevates him above the violence ignited by Ajax's corpse: "Yes, for I too shall come to this end" (1365). Odysseus' role is outside the dynamic generated by sacrifice, and his humanity and generosity function as an authorial vehicle by which Sophocles closes a conflict that has gone beyond his characters' ability to do so. Unlike the others, Odysseus is not angry, and he has not lost sight of the distinction between Ajax of old and the dead Ajax before them: "This man is an enemy, but he was once noble" (1356).

Another difference exists on stage which Menelaus and Agamemnon perceive (1047; 1231) but ignore in their rage: Ajax is dead, and they are alive. Sophocles justifies Odysseus' intervention by the theme of shared mortality (1365–67), but it is the condition of the corpse itself that re-erects differences. The accusations of the Bouphonia end with a difference and the scapegoating of the axe and knife. In *Ajax*, Ajax's corpse becomes the scapegoat; burial, the ritual expulsion from the community of one whose presence is destructive, re-establishes civilized order, for human beings bury their dead.

Thusia, Bouphonia, and *Ajax* encode an ideology that transforms the murder of animals into sacrifice. The first message is transmitted in the way of ritual: senders and receivers, performers and audience, are one and the same. Strategies of transformation always succeed since the participants are deceiving themselves. Those in the audience of Sophocles' drama, familiar as they are with myth and sacrifice, do not control what is happening before them. They are exposed to the self-trickery of their rituals. Preoccupied by their feelings for Ajax, they face, without having to admit, the guilt latent in their own pretense and hypocrisy, and experience the emotional release of Sophocles' tragic mythmaking.

Five

Patriarchal Mythmaking on Marriage

The word "marriage" denotes beliefs, customs, and kinship ties that differ from culture to culture, although we all too easily fall into the trap of assuming that the word has the same associations for everyone. To Americans today, "marriage" generally means a condition culminating a period of dating, courtship, and engagement. After the wedding, the couple constitutes a legal entity and often shares a state of holy matrimony. Love and personal choice determine the selection of a mate and remain strong forces for each partner in their lives together. Such notions of marriage, however, ill serve us in understanding Greek marriage patterns. Sex and reproduction may be drives common to all humans, but every culture imposes its own standards and conventions on how they will be satisfied. Though Athenians were monogamous, their marriage patterns are not our own.

A form of marriage practiced in Athens during the Classical period shows how far Greek customs ranged from those sketched above. This procedure, which probably grew out of purchasing a bride, was conducted sometime before the wedding by the groom and the bride's *kyrios* (master). In the presence of witnesses, the *kyrios* handed the woman over to the groom, who received her into his hands. She was entrusted by contract to the groom for the purpose of providing him with legitimate children. Accordingly, a law cited by the orator Demosthenes (384–322) states: "whatever woman the father or his brother by the same father or the grandfather on the father's side hands over to be a wife, from her are legitimate children" (*Against Stephanus B* 18). At the same time, the men established the amount and content of the dowry. A plaintiff in a suit over an unpaid dowry refers to this transaction: "I will provide witnesses that Polyeuktos handed his daughter over to me on the sum of forty mnas" (Demosthenes, *Against Spudias* 6). The dowry, attached to the woman but not hers to own, supported her in her husband's house, maintained her ties with the household of her former *kyrios*, and gave her sons a share in her paternal household through inheriting its funds. Although the husband could dispose of it, the dowry remained the possession of the woman's household and had to be repaid in case of divorce or the woman's death without children.

In "giving out" the woman, the *kyrios* did not relinquish all claims to her. As Hans Julius Wolff explains, "*Ekdosis* [giving out] . . . always implies that someone gives up power over a person or thing for a specific purpose, and its effect is the transfer of rights in so far as this is required by the purpose" [p. 49]. In Wolff's example, in giving out a baby to a nurse, certain powers are transferred to the nurse by contract in order to take care of the child, "[b]ut it is at the same time understood that no definite severance of the relationship between the transferor and the object will take place" [p. 49]. The infant does not become the nurse's possession, nor does the bride the husband's. The *kyrios* let his daughter out; in effect, he leased her procreativity to a husband for the purpose of obtaining offspring for the husband's house. Even so, she remained under his mastery to the extent that she was obligated to produce a son for *his* household, should he die without an heir. The *kyrios* thus reserved the right to dissolve the marriage and take her back (Lacey, pp. 139–45). The institution of the *epiklēros*, in which the daughter was reclaimed to marry and bear a child by her dead father's nearest relative, highlights the woman's function as childbearer and object of exchange. Both men—father and husband—seek the same ends, namely, to obtain an heir and prolong the life of the house, while each exploits the dowry and woman alike to the advantage of his household. On the other hand, *aphairesis*, removal of the woman, limited the husband's power over his wife and kept her from being fully accepted into his household, at least until the birth of a son.

The wedding, prompted by anxiety over the bride's virginity, usually followed soon after the contractual arrangements. Its rituals accomplished the woman's transition from child to adult and conducted her from her *kyrios'* house to her husband's. Rarely did the bride have any say in the choice of a groom, and during the Classical period she was not required to be present for the drafting of the contract. Protected and sustained by a *kyrios*, she remained a legal minor from birth. The practice of marrying a woman in her mid-teens to a man in his thirties contributed to her exclusion from the arrangements and reinforced her submissiveness to her husband. Romantic love played no part in uniting a couple, and whatever affection might grow between them came with time and the birth of children. The wedding publicized the woman's new status but did not itself establish any legal standing. Public recognition validated the marriage when the husband lived with the woman and treated her as his wife, held her to be the mistress of his household, and acknowledged her children as his own. Marriage, for which there was no single Greek word, thus required a contract between *kyrios* and groom, the "giving out" of the bride, and cohabitation as husband and wife.

Greek marriage everywhere entailed the exchange of a woman by men. The woman free to make her own arrangements was a prostitute or concubine, never a wife. By giving and receiving a woman, Athenian men established enduring ties and saw to the future of their houses and city. The woman lacked all rights over herself and gained no corresponding control over the men.

In 451, a law of Pericles restricted citizenship to those born of Athenian parents. Pericles apparently intended to impose limits upon eligibility for Athenian citizenship by debarring children of an Athenian father and a foreign mother [Patterson, p. 106]. The law concurred with Athenian conceptions and arrogance about the purity of their stock and national identity and intensified the dynamics of founding marriage on the outsider. The woman's situation became crucial for the husband's household. Should she be proven a foreigner or an adulteress, her children would be disenfranchised, and the house, deprived of its heir, imperiled with extinction. Consequently, the *polis* took extensive note of the composition and perpetuation of its households, allowing any qualified citizen to bring criminal indictment against a foreigner living with an Athenian as his wife or against an Athenian passing off a foreign woman as a citizen.

Greek women lived in a patriarchy in which fathers had power over mothers and children, and husbands over wives. Although essential to society, women had no say in its public, political, and economic life. Only in fertility cults and the offices of priestesses did they participate in affairs of the city. Yet, even in these, women functioned less as citizens than as avatars of the earth. They were valued here as elsewhere for their fertility, so that their inclusion in the religious sphere is consistent with their exclusion from those areas not based on reproductivity. Women were simultaneously part of and apart from the *polis*, whose ideal remained the male warrior, the *hoplitēs*. Hoplite warfare promoted cohesiveness among men and inculcated a spirit of equality and discipline in which women had no share, having no place in the fighting or in the exercise of citizens' rights based on enrolment in the army.

Mythmaking derived from marriage draws upon the actual circumstances of marriage as lived by Athenians. It reflects and prescribes an ideology of how the sexes should and should not interact. For the most part, since men controlled the *polis* and the mythmaking media, they defined gender roles, dictating what was acceptable for women, and described the ways that things could go amiss. Repeatedly, in all areas of life, they imposed upon women their messages of subordination according to which women must accept as "natural" their everyday inferiority to men.

Mythmaking about marriage gains its strength and plausibility from human physiology. It is given that women's bodies are more devoted to reproduction than those of men, and that women, at least in ancient Greek culture, engage in activities originating with reproduction for most of their adult lives. In *Management of the Household*, Xenophon (c. 428/7–c. 354) justifies Greek patriarchal marriage by the physical differences between the sexes. Here, Xenophon's Ischomachos is instructing his fifteen-year-old wife on her duties:

> Now in my opinion, wife, the gods seem to have devised the pair called female and male with particular insight that it be most advantageous to itself for the good of its common enterprise. First of all, so that the generations of living things might not fail, the pair lies with one another in begetting children. Secondly, from the pair is provided, for humans at any rate, the means of acquiring those who will attend their old age. Next, the way of life for humans is not, as it is for cattle, in the outdoors, but there is need of a roof. That is clear. Certainly, for humans who intend to have something to bring into the house, there is needed someone to do the outdoor work. Plowing, sowing, plant-

ing, pasturing, all these are outdoor occupations. From them come the necessities of life. There is need, in turn, when these are brought into the house, for someone to watch over and tend to the proper occupations of the house. The care of new-born children needs a house, as does the making of clothes from wool. Since both occupations, those inside and those outside, need work and attention, the god, as it seems to me, made nature accordingly: the woman's for indoor occupations and the man's for outdoor ones. He made the body and spirit of the man more able to overcome cold, heat, travel, and military service. Thus he assigned to him the outdoor occupations. Since he endowed the woman by nature with a body less able to overcome the rigors of cold, heat, travel, and military service, the god seems to me to have assigned to her the indoor tasks. Knowing that he had endowed her by nature and assigned her the rearing of new-born children, he also apportioned to her more affection for new-born babies than to the man. Since he also assigned to the woman the watching over what was brought into the house, and since he realized that for guarding, it was no loss if the soul be timid, the god apportioned a greater amount of timidity to the woman than to the man. On the other hand, knowing that there will be need for the one who has the outdoor occupations to act in defense of them, the god apportioned to the man the greater amount of courage (7.18–25).

The essential strategy of this model of marriage is to polarize men and women, defining as male the qualities necessary for the outdoors and as female those for indoor life. In each instance the preference for the male quality over that of the female is evident, although the household, Xenophon admits, needs both.

In mythmaking about marriage, the male (husband, father) is the first to encroach upon marriage. His actions, while harming the female (wife, mother, daughter), lie within his powers as *kyrios* and do not in themselves result in the collapse of order. Thus, in the *Oresteia*, the chorus of Argive elders can hail Agamemnon's victorious return from Troy and forgive his sacrifice of Iphigenia:

> Back then, when you were sending forth an army on account of Helen, you were pictured in ugly colors. You were not wielding the tiller of good sense by arousing courage in dying men through sacrifices. But now, neither from the top of my heart nor without friendship, I am well-disposed to those whose labors have proved successful (*Agamemnon* 799–806).

But the actions of the male cause the female to react and, by reacting, to exceed the place accorded her in his world. It is her deeds that undo marriage as a civilizing structure and plunge the household, and often the state, into chaos [Foley, pp. 4–5]. The ideology holds no alternative for the woman who transgresses her sex-gender limits; destruction and ruin for her man and household necessarily follow.

The *Hymn to Demeter* (seventh century) begins on this pattern but arrives exceptionally at stability through the marriage of Persephone and Hades, the god of the underworld. Marylin Arthur rightly observes that "[o]n one level Demeter's plight is . . . that of all women, who must achieve self-definition in a social and psychic world which values male attributes more highly and depreciates females" [1977, p. 8]. Yet the identity achieved by Demeter is restricted to that of mother, and by Persephone, to that of daughter. Demeter as wife and sexual being is suppressed, while Persephone enjoys sex only in a symbolic fashion. The mother's identity remains inextricably bound to her fertility, the daughter's and wife's to her accession to her father's and husband's will. In contrast, the males, Zeus and Hades, function not only as father and groom respectively but also outside marriage as lords of their separate dominions. Since in no sense does Demeter or Persephone assert an identity apart from that dictated by the male, the mythmaker can bring his story to an end different from the normal outcome of a female's quest for self-definition.

I begin to sing of lovely-haired Demeter, august goddess, and of her daughter with the slender ankles whom Aïdoneus [Hades] snatched away, and loud-thundering, far-seeing Zeus gave away. Far from Demeter of the golden sword and radiant fruits, she was playing with the deep-bosomed daughters of Oceanos, gathering flowers, roses, crocuses, and beautiful violets, throughout the grassy meadow, irises, hyacinths, and a narcissus that Gaia, to please the Host of Many [Hades] in accord with the plans of Zeus, produced. It was a trick for the maiden with eyes like flower buds, wondrous and shining, an awesome thing for all the immortal gods and mortal men to see. From its roots grew forth a hundred blossoms fragrant with the sweetest smell. The broad sky above, the whole earth, and swell of the salt sea laughed. Astonished, she reached out with both hands to pluck the beautiful flower. The wide-wayed earth gaped through the Nysian plain where the much-receiving lord, the many-named son of Kronos, sped with his immortal horses. Seizing her against her will, he carried her off weeping in his golden chariot. She cried out shrilly, calling upon her father, highest and bravest son of Kronos. No one of the immortals and mortals heard, not even the olives with their radiant fruits, except the timid daughter of Perses, Hecate of the gleaming headband, heard from her cave, and the shining son of Hyperion, lord Helios, heard the maiden calling to her father, son of Kronos. But he sat far from the gods in the temple of many prayers, receiving beautiful sacrifices from mortal men. Against her will but in accord with Zeus's counsels, his brother, ruler over many, much-receiving, the many-named son of Kronos, took her with his immortal horses (1–32).

The opening of the hymn recalls events from a typical wedding. On the first day, the girl ended her childhood by dedicating her toys to Artemis. On the following day in the evening, she was driven with her husband to his house where her parents showered her with dates, nuts, and dried figs, a rite to quicken her fertility. Afterwards, the couple retired to the bridal chamber. In the hymn, the violence and heedlessness of the males turn these rituals into scenes of rape, deprivation, and loss.

Zeus and Hades know what is happening and effect Persephone's transfer from father to groom with brutal force. "Loud-thundering," "far-seeing," and "ruler over many" (literally, sign-giver to many) allude to their power to define and control realms outside marriage. The females are confined within its dictates. Persephone, unaware of her *ekdosis*, is playing like a girl in a flower-sprinkled meadow, the image for the brevity of her youth and virginity. Unlike the human bride who puts away her toys knowing that her childhood is at an end, Persephone reaches out for the narcissus and is tricked into adulthood. Her cries of "father" underscore her impotence and ignorance. Hades' chariot and steeds symbolize the husband's exploitation of the bride's body, while the ride to his house suggests that marriage brings the death of the virgin. Left to Demeter are sorrow and loss. Euripides' Clytemnestra voices the outrage of the mother deprived of her part in her daughter's wedding:

Agamemnon	I will give out your child among the Argives.
Clytemnestra	Where should I be at that time?
Agamemnon	Go to Argos and care for your daughters.
Clytemnestra	Leave my child? Who will lift the marriage torch?
Agamemnon	I will supply what light befits the wedding.
Clytemnestra	No, that is not custom. Do not take it lightly.
Agamemnon	You should not stay amid the army.
Clytemnestra	I am her mother, and I should give her out.

Agamemnon	It is not right to leave our daughters alone.
Clytemnestra	They are well-guarded in the maiden chambers.
Agamemnon	Obey....
Clytemnestra	(*cutting him off*) By the Argive queen and goddess, you take care of things outside, and I those inside (*Iphigenia at Aulis* 729–40).

Clytemnestra no more than Demeter knows her *kyrios'* plans. She insists upon the male's division of the sexes and conforms to his definitions of space and knowledge. To no avail. Hecate shut away in her cave exemplifies the ideal condition of the married woman, and Demeter will have to supplicate Helios, whose sight in the myth's sexualization of perception gains information denied Hecate's hearing.

Demeter leaves Olympus and goes to Eleusis in Attica. A day's walk northwest of Athens, Eleusis remained independent of her neighbor to the south until about 600. The failure of the hymn to mention Athens leads scholars to place the date of its composition in the late seventh century. From the Mycenaean era, Eleusis was the site of a mystery cult of "the [two] goddesses," the "Demeters," "Mother and Maiden" [Parke, pp. 55–72]. Mysteries (*my-* to shut one's mouth) denote things said and done about which the initiate must keep mum. Nonetheless, much is known about the rituals from allusions, which were permitted, like those in the hymn to Demeter's arrival and sojourn in Celeus' house. The central rites, however, remained secret, despite the cult's longevity. (It survived to c. A.D. 400.) To judge from lines 480–82 of the hymn, the Mysteries did not confer immortality or rebirth but offered a better lot for the initiated in the lower world: "Blessed of men on earth is he who has seen [the Mysteries]. He who is uninitiated in the holy rites and has no part of them does not have a portion of like blessedness, once he is dead in the dank darkness."

Within the dynamics of mythmaking, Demeter's flight to Eleusis substitutes for direct retaliation against the male, the usual response in myths about women. On earth, where she is protected by her divinity, Demeter can be a sign-giver. Her tale of Cretan pirates, though a lie and therefore consistent with the perversion of male language by females, points to reconciliation. "I escaped those arrogant rulers so that those who carried me unpaid far across the sea might not profit from my price" (131–32). Demeter would willingly give up Persephone, she implies, if properly compensated. During her brief stay on earth, she bestows rites that permanently alter the human condition and mollify the sufferings of humans. In her wrath and despite herself, Demeter serves Zeus in the way of Hesiod's Hecate. On the other hand, Metaneira replicates Hesiod's Woman. Demeter seeks to make Metaneira's son Demophoön ageless and immortal by burning away his mortal parts in the fire. Interrupted by his terrified mother, Demeter rebukes the woman: "Men are foolish and without thought who cannot foresee the portion of good or evil yet to come. By your foolishness, you have erred beyond any cure" (256–58). However, Metaneira does not react out of ignorance but from mother love, that affection "endowed her by nature," according to Xenophon, and viewed by the ideology as instinctive in women. Her deed explains why the rites do not confer immortality. The same force that prompts her to intervene condemns her child to mortality. A female once again deprives men of deathlessness.

Demeter vents her anger and longing for Persephone upon men:

> Across the fertile land, Demeter made a most dreadful and cruel year. The earth did not send forth any seed, for well-wreathed Demeter kept it hidden. In vain, the oxen dragged the curved ploughs over the fields, and uselessly

much white barley fell upon the earth. Then, the race of
speaking men would have perished utterly and deprived
those who have homes on Olympus of sacrifices had not
Zeus discerned and pondered in his mind (305–13).

Men suffer in place of Zeus, as the strategy of substitution
averts open conflict. Concerned for his sacrifices, whose
importance is established at the outset of the hymn, Zeus
sends Iris to Demeter. He cannot force her to stop the
famine because he has no sway over the earth's fertility.
His helplessness, glossed over by stressing the failure of
Iris and the other gods to persuade Demeter, reveals the
underbelly of sex-gender mythmaking: one sex can be
made dominant only by blurring qualities of the other. We
saw how Hesiod gave Zeus trickery in order to enable his
Zeus to deceive Metis. Another conspicuous example occurs in the *Hymn to Aphrodite* (date uncertain), where the
poet lauds Aphrodite's ability to stir "sweet desire in gods"
and to subdue "the throng of mortal men, hovering birds,
and all the beasts" (2–4). He then has Zeus "throw into
her the sweet desire to mate with a mortal" (45–46). The
hymn tells the myth of Aphrodite's humiliation through
intercourse with Trojan Anchises, by whom she becomes
the mother of Aeneas. But Aphrodite cannot be inspired
with the desire she herself embodies. The mythmaker, to
humble Aphrodite and incorporate her into the cosmos
ruled by Zeus, has to violate the logic of his own system,
a necessity which exposes that most potent of deities,
Aphrodite.

Having failed to move Demeter through Iris, Zeus sends
Hermes to Hades, over whom, as the dominant male, he
has influence. "Aïdoneus, lord of the lower world, smiled
with furrowed brows and did not disobey the commands
of king Zeus" (357–58). Rape moves toward marriage when
Hades explains to "prudent Persephone" (359) what honors and privileges she will receive as his wife. The epithet

daïphrōn, normally descriptive of men, concedes to Persephone the good sense to see the value of Hades' offer, but it also implies that she has no thoughts apart from those of the male.

Upon hearing Hades' offer of gifts and his order that she return to Demeter, "wise Persephone laughed and quickly leaped from joy" (370–71). Is this joy over seeing her mother or over the rewards just promised? The poet is playfully ambivalent. Later, when Persephone tells her mother about the pomegranate seed, he provides a clue to his meaning. The pomegranate is a round, red fruit, filled with edible seeds and red juice. Here, it symbolizes sexual fertility and the consummation of the marriage.

> Hades gave her a pomegranate seed to eat in secret, resolving that she not remain all her days there beside revered Demeter of the dark veil (371–74).

However, when Demeter asks, "Daughter, did you eat any food while you were below?" (393–94), Persephone embellishes what happened:

> Secretly, he gave me a pomegranate seed, honey-sweet food, and compelled me by force against my will to eat it (411–13).

Hades deceives Hermes; the agent of Zeus presumably would return Persephone to her mother intact. Persephone's joy is for marriage whose fruits are honeyed, while Demeter relinquishes her wrath after regaining her daughter for two-thirds of the year. They are joined by Hecate and Rhea, and together the goddesses return to Olympus. The final scene "expresses a female solidarity which is discovered in the context of a patriarchal world" [Arthur, 1977, p. 30]. The goddesses find comfort by identifying with one another in the continuum of mother giving birth to daughter upon which the male endeavor depends.

In the poet's solution, rape becomes marriage through the honors given the daughter and respect conferred upon the mother. By defining Persephone's prudence in male terms, his mythmaking robs her of it, and deprives her of freedom of choice by willing her desire for marriage and her mother's acquiescence once her daughter has "eaten" with Hades. The "ruined" outcast becomes a legitimate wife upon accepting her rapist as husband. The solidarity exemplified by Demeter and Persephone comes at the cost of a crushing, stifling loss of self. Phyllis Chesler's observation in *Women and Madness* manifests the subtext, the obverse of Persephone's joy and compliance, that resides in the myth's message:

> Persephone, like her mother, is denied uniqueness, individuality, and cultural potency. Neither Demeter nor Persephone is allowed to become a "heroine": one represents the earth, the other represents a return to earth. Their single fate symbolizes the inevitable, endless breaking of each individual woman on the wheel of biological reproduction [p. 263].

All of us renew the ancient world from our individual perspectives. Chesler interprets the myth as a modern feminist with her sense of self and her independent ambitions. Ancient Greek women, to speak for the silent dead, accustomed to their circumstances, probably did not on the whole share her desires nor feel her deprivation in Persephone and Demeter. Her insight, nevertheless, has value, for it voices the repression presupposed by the myth. In the household of Celeus and Metaneira, the husband goes outside to join other men in maintaining the city "by their plans and straight judgments" (152), the wife manages everything within the house, the daughters are ready for marriage, and the son— "late born, much prayed for, and welcome" (165)—is the focus that imparts meaning to all. As in Hesiod, this mythmaking on marriage appropriates the useful in its construct of Woman—the virginal daughter, the subservient wife, the fertile mother of sons—and deems anything else excessive, an unwanted addition that causes the breakdown of order. The paradigm leaves out much because it compartmentalizes the sexes by gender roles. It predicates no crossing over. Husband, wife, daughters, son—each fulfills a discrete social role. But individuals do not live in compartments. Sterile and impotent alone, they release energy by mingling, corrupting their purity by social and sexual intercourse. "Dirt," to use Edmund Leach's term [p. 62], aptly describes the loss of order brought about by commingling.

The exchange of women, at least in the mythmaking imagination, was indeed a dirty business. In a society of households jealous of their independence and suspicious of women, men nonetheless had to give out and take in daughters. Only Zeus keeps his daughter, Hestia, at home to attend his hearth, but myths of gods transcend the rules limiting men. More perilous than sending out a daughter is bringing another man's daughter into the house. Wives, even the steadfast Penelope, are not to be trusted. The Homeric Clytemnestra yields willingly to the seducer Aegisthus, who slays Agamemnon on his return from war. "Nothing is more dreadful or lower," Agamemnon tells Odysseus in the underworld, "than a woman who ponders such deeds. An unseemly act she devised who worked slaughter for her wedded husband" (11.427–30). The warning from the dead Agamemnon that Odysseus not tell his wife everything makes sense coming from him, although, he adds, "You, Odysseus, will never be murdered by your wife" (11.444). On the other hand, Athena cautions Odysseus' son Telemachus to speed home at once:

> You know what sort of spirit is in a woman's breast. She
> wants to aid the house of that man who marries her. No
> longer does she remember her earlier children and dear
> husband when he is dead or have thought for him (15.20–
> 23).

Athena voices an attitude toward women prevalent also
in the Classical period. The woman, brought into the house
as wife, never fully belongs to that man and his household.
Athena intimates to Telemachus that another man may
succeed in winning Penelope, even naming Eurymachos
whom Penelope's father and brothers are urging her to
marry since he surpasses the others in giving gifts. Telemachus gleans her meaning and excuses himself from Menelaus' hospitality with the not-so-false pretext that he fears
in his absence he may lose "something precious" from his
house (15.91).

Athenian architects built in the bricks and limestone
stucco of the typical house an image of space which represents the equation of women with the inside and men
with the outside and suggests that women are precious
things to be protected [Pomeroy, p. 80; Gould, p. 48;
Walker, pp. 81–91; Keuls, 210–15]. Most women spent
most of their lives within a house whose perimeter was
broken by a single door opening onto the street. Like the
walls of the city, the house enclosed and defended women
from intruders. Sequestered within its recesses or on the
second floor, they lived out their days in the time-con-
suming, repetitive work of weaving, cooking, caring for
children, and nursing the sick. Near the door or across the
courtyard stood the men's quarters and public rooms
where they entertained their guests. This arrangement en-
sured men control over the entrance and prevented
women from encountering men who were not relatives.
The same image underlies Ischomachos' instructions in

Xenophon's treatise and, as we shall see, the sculptors' metopes of Centaurs and Amazons on the Parthenon. In tragedies performed in the 430s, Sophocles and Euripides disassemble sexualized space by seizing on its inherent contradiction. The inside of *polis* and house, women's proper places, cannot designate the civilized, a male quality, as long as the female is associated with its opposite, the savage. Rather than gems to be guarded, women are vipers, importing the beast within civilization's defenses. Their presence destroys the exclusions of polar mythmaking, allowing the tragedians to reveal the likeness of woman to man.

Deianira in Sophocles' *The Women of Trachis* and Medea in Euripides' play of the same name breach their husband's house with the savage. They little resemble one another as dramatic characters, but Deianira's ignorance of poisons and unintentional daring presupposes Medea's knowledge of poisons and intentional daring. In any case, the actions of one parallel those of the other, because both rehearse the dangers of a woman in the house. Each woman abides by the marriage until wronged by her husband. Heracles, overcome by passion for the beautiful Iole, destroys her father's city and sends her home to his wife to watch over until his return. Jason, for his part, divorces Medea without informing her and marries the daughter of the king of Corinth.

Deianira reacts first with sympathy for the ill-fated Iole. Even after she discovers Heracles' intention, she understands how he could succumb to sexual passion:

> Whoever stands up to come to blows, like a boxer, with Eros has no sense. He rules over the gods as he wishes, and me, too. Why not other women like me? I would be crazy to blame my husband, caught by this sickness, or the woman who has caused me no shame or evil (441–48).

Later, however, aroused by indignation—"And now we two wait under the bedsheet to be taken into his arms" (539–40). . . . How could any woman live in the same house with her, sharing the same marriage?" (545–46)—and by the desire to keep him, she resorts to the Centaur's charm to define herself as Heracles' wife.

Ferrying Heracles' new wife Deianira across a river, the Centaur Nessus fondled her lustfully. Heracles, in response to her scream, shot and fatally wounded Nessus with an arrow dipped in the poison of the Hydra's blood. As he lay dying, the Centaur told the young girl:

> Child of old Oeneus, if you obey me you will profit from my ferrying, since you are the last I have brought across. If you take the blood clotted around my wound, where the serpent of Lerna dipped its dark poisons, you will have a charm over Heracles, so that he will never look at another woman or love any more than you (569–77).

Deianira brings the beast's charm into Heracles' house. "I kept it safe," she tells the chorus of Trachinian women, "like the writing on a bronze tablet that cannot be washed away" (682–83). The word for tablet, *deltos,* suggests the letter delta, whose upper-case pyramid form alludes to the female body [DuBois, 1979, pp. 41–42]. Deianira has retained the poison in the recesses of Heracles' house and, symbolically, in his wife's intimate regions. She does not comprehend the ambiguity of the beast's words nor question, until too late, his motives for aiding her. She smears the robe with poison to lure Heracles from the younger woman to herself. Competitive spirit and passion valued in a man become daring in a woman, even in a woman like Deianira who "knows her place."

> I cannot fathom or understand daring, bad women. I loathe women who have acted daringly. If somehow I can surpass

this young thing with my love spells and charms on Heracles, the deed is done, unless I seem to be acting rashly. If so, I will stop (582–87).

Deianira violates the marriage by sending the robe outside the house. Dispensation of property belongs to the male. She plans badly; the result could not be otherwise when woman exceeds her place. She becomes Medea.

Medea, who had "helped Jason in every way" (13), reacts to his betrayal with violence. "She hates the children," the nurse warns, "she is not gladdened to see them. I fear she is planning something dreadful (36–37). . . . For she is dreadful, and whoever falls into enmity with her will not easily carry off the victory" (44–45). Medea plots her vengeance. She fawns upon Creon to get a day's reprieve from his decree of banishment and chooses, after deliberation, to poison the king, Jason, and his bride. "Best to go the straightest way, in which I am very skilled, to destroy them by poisons" (384–85). After hearing from Aegeus the importance of children to men, she resolves to slay her children by Jason. Her motives are those of the man and warrior:

> Let no one think me of no account, weak, and passive, but of the opposite sort, harsh on enemies and gentle to friends (807–9).

The Athenian lawgiver and poet Solon includes the same wish in his prayer for the good things of life.

> Grant me wealth in accord with the gods and to have always a good reputation among men and to be sweet to friends and bitter to enemies (fr. 1).

Deianira dies alone on Heracles' bed, pierced with his sword, her marriage become a violent perversion of Eros.

Impelled by the same passions that drive Heracles, she situates herself outside her roles of wife and mother. "Why should she nourish the dignity of the name mother," her son Hyllus asks, "when she acts in no way like one who has given birth?" (817–18). Outside the house, Heracles ironically comes closest to Deianira: "Now I am discovered a wretched woman" (1075). But there is no real irony; Heracles weeps "like a girl" (1071–72) in an approximation of the sexes that can only occur in the liminal zone demarcated by death beds separate and apart.

Both Deianira and Heracles destroy the house, and both act to restore it. In the final scene, the repulsion Hyllus feels for Iole mirrors the brutality of his father's demands. Yet Heracles renews the household and reestablishes order by giving Iole in marriage to his son. Moreover, in administering the Centaur's poisoned blood, Deianira, no less than Heracles, cures the house of its sickness, its excessive lust, and erotic passions, and allows for its restoration. The tragedy of Sophocles' play comes out of human emotions too strong to be contained by human institutions.

Medea commits the horrific, almost unimaginable, crime of killing her own children to punish Jason and to keep from being mocked by her enemies. "No Greek woman would ever have dared do that" (1339), Jason charges, naming her a lioness and a Scylla with "a savage nature" (1342–43). In the last scene, Medea appears above Jason's house; she is mounted in the chariot of Helios and has the dead bodies of their children with her. Euripides' ending, as fantastic as it is puzzling, seems intended to shock the audience with the god's acceptance of Medea. Does it suggest that Medea's acts are justified, even the slaying of her children? From the censure of the murders by the Corinthian women of the chorus, that appears unlikely. At the least, Medea culminates her vengeance by denying Jason burial of his children, while Euripides shatters sex-gender mythmaking through a woman who successfully wreaks vengeance upon her man.

In the introduction to this study, we cautioned that defining a myth may itself become a mythmaking activity. Words spent on verbal constructs create new constructs, and interpreters of a text transform it into different but related texts which differ from the original to the degree that the critics, guided and constrained by their tastes, assumptions, and perspectives, and by their purpose, medium, and audience, choose to emphasize and/or omit certain things. Critics invest a text with new meaning by looking at its language in a different way. "What does it mean?" "Why has no one seen that before, if it's *in* the play?" are questions predicated on the presumption that meaning is like gold, undoubtedly valuable and waiting to be dug out. "Meaning," however, is the sense that spectator, reader, and critic make of the text and can communicate to others willing to listen. A reading of Sophocles' *Oedipus the King* from a Freudian approach might not find a kind reception among philologists nor might a philologist's among Freudians.

The telling or reading of a myth or a critic's transformation of it necessarily affects its receptors, who are predisposed either to accept or reject its messages. Those who reject them react in ways that are not conducive to group solidarity; they may even form rival groups. On the other hand, supportive members of an audience may disagree over individual points of a text or the comparative value of readings, but they generally concur in how the myth or transformation should be expounded. About 492, the tragic poet Phrynikos went beyond his audience's expectations in writing a play about the capture of Miletus by the Persians (494). Athenians complained that it grieved them to recall the recent sufferings of friends. They fined the poet one thousand drachmas and banned the play.

Members of an audience, "an interpretative community," to borrow Stanley Fish's expression, share the same paradigm of the text's meaning. They agree on what it *can* say and, therefore, on what questions may be legitimately asked of it [Fish, pp. 338–55]. Thus, the story told by critics about the *Oresteia*, for example, acts as a myth that both exemplifies and shapes a culture. These transformations go beyond the *Oresteia* by talking about it, adding to it, altering it. In their own right, they become words in action in classrooms, journals, and books, and in the popular media.

In *Eumenides*, Aeschylus transfers the venue of myth-making from the limited range of human possibility to the freedoms of the gods, and transcends the mortal realm of Argos to the liminal zone of the Acropolis at Athens. Midway between sacred Olympus above and the profane city below, the Acropolis affords space where gods and men interact to reorganize the "house" of Athens. Critics have long admired these scenes for depicting "the establishment of justice for western civilization" [Munich, p. 251]. In an innovative study, "The Dynamics of Misogyny: Myth and Mythmaking in the *Oresteia*," Froma I. Zeitlin changed the paradigm of what is acceptable to say about the *Oresteia*. For her, the work becomes a "gynocentric document," one founded on the female, that discovers male order by subjugating and controlling the female: "the basic issue in the trilogy is the establishment in the face of female resistance of the binding nature of patriarchal marriage where wife's subordination and patrilineal succession are reaffirmed" [p. 149]. The consequences of Zeitlin's feminist perspective entail far more than different meanings for the text. The discourse of previous critics comes under scrutiny as a kind of meta-*Oresteia* that supplements the original by explaining the plays through its own constructs. Ultimately, the meta-text fuses with and replaces the original, and mythmaking by critics becomes synonymous with and masquerades as Aeschylus' mythmaking. Indeed, Adrienne Munich minces no words in asserting that "[c]ritical discourse has tended to be more misogynist than the texts it examines. Tagged with patriarchal interpretation, canonical texts pass into the culture validated by what the Institution of Reading has understood. How many of us, for example, were taught that the *Oresteia* is about the establishment of justice for Western civilization, rather than that it is a great act of mythopoeia in which politics are sexualized and where the idea of justice becomes defined as 'masculine'?" [p. 251].

In 458, Aeschylus won the prize at the Great Dionysia with his *Oresteia*. The work originally consisted of three tragedies, *Agamemnon*, *The Libation Bearers*, and *Eumenides*, and a satyr-play, *Proteus*. The latter, a farce or burlesque on Menelaus' encounter in Egypt with the polymorphic god of the sea, has been lost. The remaining plays offer a powerful dramatization of the dirty business of exchanging women in marriage. Agamemnon has brought into his house Tyndareus' daughter Clytemnestra. In his absence at Troy, she takes a lover, assumes the power in his city, and, upon his return, slays him. In the final moments of *The Libation Bearers*, their son Orestes, who has just killed his mother, voices in a prayer the primal scream of mythmaking on marriage:

> May no such woman ever live with me in my house.
> Sooner, may I die at the gods' hands childless (1005–6).

Eumenides offers Athenians the fantasy that they can escape having to bring a woman into their "house" of Athens.

The discussion that follows analyzes not only Aeschylus' mythmaking on marriage but also the still potent patriarchal myth long told about these scenes. We do not claim to have the one truth about Aeschylus' mythmaking nor to be free ourselves of a particular perspective. To begin, we quote as a representative text of the patriarchal reading a summary of the trial from a standard history of Greek literature published in 1960:

> The scene now changes to Athens, where Athena summons the Areios Pagos to judge the matter. The Erinyes press the charge against Orestes; Apollo bears testimony in his favour, and raises the curious plea that son and mother are not really akin, the father being the only true parent. The votes of the court are equally divided, and Athena gives the casting-vote in Orestes' favour. She then calms the rage of the baffled chorus and induces them to remain in Athens as beneficent powers, henceforth to be called Eumenides (Kindly goddesses), not Erinyes. The trilogy ends with a solemn procession escorting them to the shrine which was theirs in historical times [Rose, p. 156].

At *Eumenides* 397, Orestes and the Erinyes stand before Athena on the Areopagus, a low hill northwest of the Acropolis. The goddess asks who they are and what the matter is between them. "We are the everlasting children of Night" (416); we drive murderers from houses" (421); "he deigned to be his mother's slayer" (425). "Did he fear the wrath of some other necessity?" Athena inquires (426). The Erinyes deem no motive sufficient for matricide and reproach Orestes for refusing to swear an oath to his innocence. Since he admits the deed (462–64), Orestes cannot take such an oath, and the Erinyes consider that conclusive of their claim on him. Athena responds, "Do you wish to be just in reputation or do you want to act justly?"

Erinyes How is that? Instruct us. You are not deficient in wisdom.
Athena I say do not let the unjust prevail by oaths.

> *Erinyes* Well, question him, and give a straight judgment.
> *Athena* Would you entrust the outcome of the accusation
> to me?
> *Erinyes* Certainly. We respect you and receive respect in
> return (430–35).

Gilbert Murray expresses the patriarchal reading of the Erinyes' concession of their case to Athena:

> And what exactly is the change that has taken place in the Furies, to explain this change of attitude in the play? It is that they have given up their claim for a purely mechanical working of the Law that the Doer must Suffer, and have accepted Athena's principle that not only the deed shall be considered but everything that caused or surrounded the deed. They accept *peithous sebas* [awe for persuasion], the sanctity of the spirit which persuades and hears Persuasion; that is, they will listen to Persuasion and will think again. They become no longer a mechanical Law of Retribution which operates blindly; but a Law which thinks and feels and seeks real Justice [pp. 203–4].

Murray's language endows the Erinyes with changes in attitude that are not expressed in the text, and he ignores the presence of the author. While the dramatic situation— "he deigned to be his mother's slayer" (425)—leaves no doubt that the Erinyes believe they will defeat Orestes, the respect they grant Athena has no dramatic justification and constitutes an authorial intrusion. With one question, "Did he fear the wrath of some other necessity?" (426), Athena does introduce a new and enlightened concept of justice, namely, that of extenuating circumstances, a concept treasured by patriarchal criticism, but one which she ultimately ignores. With another question, "Would you entrust the outcome of the accusation to me?" (434), Aeschylus takes an essential step in solving the problem of the female.

In her preliminary examination, Athena plays the role

of the king archon at the council of the Areopagus, the magistrate responsible for determining whether contesting parties had grounds for an action before that body. The council, called the Areopagus from its seat on the hill (*pagus*) of Ares, had from earliest times heard cases of homicide. Recent legislation (462/61) had reorganized the council, stripping it of its political powers and restricting its activities to religious affairs, which included homicide. The reforms cost their instigator Ephialtes his life and surely continued to stir passions among Athenians, thus affording the *Oresteia* contemporary significance.

Athena declares the matter beyond the competence of mortals to judge, nor "is it right for me to decide between cases of murder sharp to arouse anger" (471–72). She sets up a court, and Aeschylus capitalizes on the topicality of the Areopagus' structure to lend the aura of a foundation myth to his dramaturgy:

> Since this matter has fallen here, I will choose sworn judges of murder and establish a tribunal, one for all time to come. You [Erinyes and Orestes], summon your witnesses and evidence, helpful supports for your cases. I will select the best of my citizens and return, literally, to decide this matter (482–88).

Through the trial, Aeschylus transposes the problem of the female from a social conflict between the sexes into a judicial and political issue. Concerning such issues the men of the jury can determine what they want. Erinyes become prosecutors, Orestes the defendant with Apollo as advocate, and Athena the presiding judge who establishes procedures in the course of the trial. The jurors get to decide not only Orestes' case but also that of the Erinyes and Clytemnestra.

The Erinyes hound Orestes because he has shed kin blood. They deny the effectiveness of Apollo's purificatory rites; they smell out Orestes by the drops of blood (247). In accord with their ancient privilege, he is theirs:

> This portion unchanging Fate spun out for me to have perpetually: to pursue those mortals upon whom it has fallen to do wanton murders until he goes underground. Even dead, he is not very free (333–40).

They shift from a plural to a singular subject as their thoughts move from general rule to Orestes himself. He has no legal defense against them, but they have exposed themselves to Athena's wisdom and persuasion. By entrusting their case to her, they also entrust it to Zeus, whose wisdom is synonymous with Athena's. Male wisdom is about to judge the problem of the female *with her consent*.

Aeschylus previews the nature of justice at the court in his version of the name Areopagus. Tradition attributes it to the trial of Ares for murdering Halirrothios. According to Apollodorus,

> Halirrothios, son of Poseidon and the nymph Eurutes, attempts to rape Alcippe, daughter of Agraulos and Ares. Ares finds him out and slays him. Poseidon indicts him on the Areopagus with the twelve gods as judges. Ares is tried and acquitted (*Library* 3.14.2).

Aeschylus opts for, perhaps invents, an etiology for the name that emphasizes violence over judicial procedure and subjugation of the female over dispensation of justice:

> This is the hill of Ares, where the Amazons pitched their tents when they came with an army in spite toward Theseus and built towers against this new, lofty-towered city. They sacrificed to Ares, thus giving his name to the rock (685–90).

Theseus' defeat of the Amazon invaders assures male control over Athens. Athena accomplishes the same end through her court, as she implies in Aeschylus' ambivalent line 488: "I return, literally, to decide this matter." *Etétymōs*, Greek for "literally," signals an etymology so that the word for "decide" (*diairein*) assumes the full weight of its components, which mean "to take apart." Not only does Athena hint that she, rather than the jurors, will decide the case, but also that the grip the Erinyes have upon Orestes will be severed.

The Erinyes begin by cross-examining Orestes, who admits his guilt. Clytemnestra has "two strokes of pollution upon her," he contends, "for she killed her husband and my father" (600; 602). He presses the Erinyes, "Why did you not drive her into exile, when she was alive?" (604). Their reply, "She was not of the same blood as the man she slew" (605), elicits from Orestes the central question which, more than his case, it is the function of the court to resolve: "Am I of my mother's blood?" (606). The Erinyes respond with what appears to be the incontrovertible fact of human existence: "Of course. Did she not nourish you beneath her girdle? Are you repudiating the dearest blood of your mother?" (607–8). Orestes was carried beneath Clytemnestra's girdle. If that signifies Clytemnestra's motherhood, then Orestes cannot escape. But Aeschylus shifts the issue to the *blood link* between mother and son. If it can be shown that the son is not of his mother's blood, then, despite the fact that Clytemnestra carried him, he killed her in righteous vengeance for slaying his true parent, the father. From this point of view, Apollo's denial of the mother as parent is far from "curious."

Orestes resigns his defense to Apollo, who proves to be a bungling advocate. Apollo first tries to impress the jury with his authority as Zeus's prophet. The murder was just, because Zeus favors the father, an argument that runs aground on the contradiction pointed out by the Erinyes. If Zeus so favors the father, why did he shackle his own father Kronos? Apollo's rejoinder, that fetters can be loosened but "whenever the dust soaks up a man's blood, once he is dead, there is no raising up" (647–48), reaffirms the Erinyes' contention: "The mother's blood on the ground is hard to bring up" (261–62). "Bungling," however, may be too strong. Apollo has no defense to plea or testimony to offer. He cites, instead, a theory of embryology:

> The mother is not the one called the parent of the child but the nurse of the newly-sown seed. The one who mounts is the parent. A stranger, she preserves a stranger's young plant for those whom the god does no harm (658–61).

For proof of his "science," Apollo directs the jurors' attention to Athena, whom "no goddess could have produced" (666). Her presence confirms his contention, which is never refuted. Apollo concludes by attempting to bribe the jurors with an alliance between Athens and Orestes' city of Argos. Meta-mythmaking trivializes Apollo's science into sophistry, clever and subtle argumentation with hints of deception and insincerity. Apollo, patriarchal myth says, cannot be serious; Aeschylus simply needs something for Orestes' advocate to advocate. In fact, Apollo converts to scientific terms the Athenians' ancient belief in their autochthony;* both posit an escape from the mother as parent, denying her participation in procreativity. Apollo's theory also coincides with the democracy's restriction of meaning-making to the male, since the latter forms the child, while the female passively receives his seed/sign.

---

*Autochthony denotes birth from the earth (*chthon-*) itself (*auto-*) rather than birth from a woman and a man.

Despite Rose's assertion that "The votes of the court are equally divided, and Athena gives the casting-vote in Orestes' favour" [156], the sole indicators for how this scene was played are the words of the script. Stage directions have been inserted by translators and lack ancient authority. To interpret the crucial voting scene (711–41), we therefore adopt Oliver Taplin's principle that "significant stage action is implicit in the text . . . *all* the action *necessary* for a viable and comprehensible production of a Greek tragedy is, as a matter of fact, included in the words" [p. 17].

At *Eumenides* 566, Athena returns with her jurors. Aeschylus does not mention their number; the audience could see for itself how many there were. The jurors probably sit on benches until the goddess calls for them to cast their votes and decide the case (709–10). The Erinyes, who are the prosecutors, follow with a couplet (711–12); one juror, we assume, approaches the urn for condemnation and drops in his pebble. The advocate Apollo speaks two lines (713–14), and one juror casts his pebble for acquittal. The Erinyes pronounce five couplets and one final triplet for six condemning votes, while Apollo pronounces five couplets for five acquitting votes. The human jury condemns Orestes. Despite Apollo's support and the heinousness of Clytemnestra's crime, they decide for the mother, gainsaying the male's right to dispose of the female at will. So strong is the tie of mother-blood. The jurors feel it, and so does H.J. Rose, who considers Apollo's denial "curious" in his summary.

The Erinyes' triplet gives Athena time to move downstage:

> My task is to decide the case last. I shall add this pebble for Orestes. No mother bore me. I praise the male in all things, save in being married, with all my spirit. I am exceedingly the father's. I shall not hold in greater esteem

the lot of a woman who killed the man, overseer of the house. Orestes wins if the votes be judged equal (734–41).

With the words, "I shall add this pebble," Athena drops a pebble into the urn for acquittal. Hers is the last vote, but it is not the deciding vote cast by a presiding officer when the ballot turns out equal. The difference is crucial. The goddess *ties* the voting; six against five becomes six to six [Gargarin, p. 127]. Athena's concern for circumstances in the preliminary examination proves a sham; she asserts not a judgment but the priority of the male and father. She both decides the matter and severs the Erinyes' grip. At the same time, she rescues the human jurors from their scruple about the mother with its disastrous consequences for the social order. Orestes wins his case; by implication, Clytemnestra is neither his mother nor Iphigenia's.

The scene calls for eleven jurors; Rose assumes twelve. The latter belief, promoted by English-speaking scholars, cannot but reflect their own judicial system. "Twelve honest men have decided the cause," wrote Sir William Pulteney, Earl of Bath, in 1731. The metaphor of a British judiciary familiarizes and unifies the scene. The reader circumvents the specter of Orestes' rejection by the jury and the triumph of the Erinyes' "mechanical" justice over Athena's enlightenment. The transition from blindness to "real" justice, to "a Law which thinks and feels," unimperiled by the jurors' decision, occurs serenely. But in a different telling of the transition, order yields to disorder and the certainty of the "Doer must Suffer" to the profound disputes of litigants. In a third telling, the transition is from a view of the world that has become insufficient and therefore female to a more perfect hierarchy.

The metaphor also leads to an idea of divinity comparable to the Christian deity. In Murray's words,

> Athena is the daughter of Zeus, created by him alone, with no mother. She is 'completely the Father's,' pure undiluted Zeus (738, 826). And she acquits the prisoner.
> This conception of a God who is above the Law and therefore forgiving is the great contribution made to the religion of Europe by Greek anthropomorphism [p. 201].

Rather than a goddess born from Zeus's head, a figment of mythology, Athena becomes "the daughter of the father" and casts a vote no longer based on naked prejudice and the bizarre circumstances of her birth. Instead, she dispenses mercy and forgiveness, having afforded the Erinyes due consideration. Athena, to be sure, is Zeus's daughter, but in the phrase "the daughter of Zeus" she performs a role analogous to the Son of the Father in redeeming the prisoner, himself a substitute for all men. There is nothing in Aeschylus' text about forgiveness. It exists only in the critic's mythmaking, in his urge for a "better" ending.

The verdict ends the trial and the Erinyes' suit for justice. But the Erinyes are enraged over the injury they perceive to their ancient prerogative by the release of Orestes. Athena persuades them to relinquish their wrath and accept a home in her city. A procession, led by the goddess, escorts them to their chambers on the side of the Acropolis. For chambers, Aeschylus uses *thalamoi* (1004), which denotes the women's quarters of the house. His Athena introduces the virgin daughters of Night into the "household" of Athens. Their dowry, the first fruits of the harvest and sacrifices for weddings and births, is offered them by the people of Attica.

Athena proclaims that "Zeus of the Agora has prevailed" (973). Zeus Agoraios, A.W. Verrall explains, refers to "the Supreme Power, which favours *civility*, reason and moderation" [pp. 169–70]. The agora formed the symbolic center of the *polis* where citizens congregated as equals.

The social space [of the agora] was a centered space—common, public, egalitarian, and symmetrical—but also secularized, intended for confrontation, debate, and argument [Vernant, 1982, p. 126].

Such speech, by definition and by the realities of the agora, is male. In the *Eumenides, his* voice civilizes the Erinyes by integrating them into the cosmos verbalized by men. It talks away their undesirable wrath and appropriates their fertility for the land, women, and animals of the men of Attica. In the end, it deprives the Angry Ones (Erinyes) of their identity by renaming them the Kindly Ones (Eumenides), whose kindness, unlike their anger, benefits others.

On stage, appearances would belie any connection between the Olympian warrior goddess, clad in her aegis, and the throng of gorgon-like creatures eager to eat Orestes alive (305). But Athena, virgin warrior and motherless daughter of the father, and the Erinyes, fertility virgins and fatherless daughters of the mother, are complements. Together they represent the daughter who is dutiful to her father and whose fertility is available to him without his having to give her away in marriage. Aeschylus patterns his construct of Athena/Erinyes after the *epiklēros,* the woman who, when her father dies without a male heir, is married to her nearest paternal relative so that the son of that union, the father's grandson, may inherit his property. In so far as the purpose of the institution of the *epiklēros* was the same as that of marriage, namely, to perpetuate the father's house, the grandson is in effect the father's son by his own daughter. Athena reproduces the woman's loyalty to her father, and the Erinyes, her reproductivity. The Erinyes have no father, hence no allegiance to another "household," and they provide for the well-being and fertility of Athenians. They take the place of the wife, the metaphorical field for the husband's plowing. Since her functions are fulfilled by virgin spirits of the earth, the men of Athens have no need to bring a woman into their house. They are self-sufficient, free of the taint and problem of the sexed, daring woman, whose nature is foreign in physique, blood, and loyalties.

Six

Myths and Citizenship

The myths studied in this and the following chapters were told by Athenians seeking political ends. By political, we mean having to do with the relations of a citizen with other citizens and of the *polis* with other *poleis*. Mythic discourse is political in that a group of people identify themselves as related to one another and distinct from other groups by telling the same myths; even more important is the difference between how they tell them to those within and without the group. The historicity Greeks granted their myths secured for them the authority of reality without the need to seek the historian's closest approximation to what actually occurred. The truth of myths or belief in them mattered much less than their power to affect an audience. Again, myths are words put into action.

Athenians shared a *polis* which had Athens as its urban center and all of Attica as its territory. The *polis'* civic center was in the agora at Athens, and its religious center at the communal hearth somewhere near the agora in the Prytaneum. The population consisted of citizens and their children, resident aliens (metics), and slaves. Athenian men, the citizens proper, joined in public business in the council, assembly, and law courts; celebrated festivals and sacrifices before temples and in shrines; and gathered for society of all sorts in the haunts, byways, and houses of the city. The life of the state took place mainly in Athens, but local organizations spread across Attica determined who could participate. These groups, set up as their own corporations with property and a cult, were the tribe, the deme, and the phratry [Patterson, pp. 8–28; Fine, pp. 183–88; 235–38; Sealey, pp. 12–19]. In accord with their rules and procedures, sons of their constituent houses were admitted into the citizen body.

Every citizen belonged to two tribes, one defined by territory, the other by kinship. During the fifth century, the territorial tribe had existed for only a short time. In 507, the statesman Cleisthenes had divided Attica into three regions—the city and its environs, the inland, and the coast—and created ten tribes by drawing demes from each region. Each tribe, with its own cult and officials, held meetings and banquets. A statue of its eponymous hero stood in the agora at Athens beside those of the other tribes, and members rallied there for tribal news and gossip. Tribes competed among themselves for honors in serving the people, particularly in the choral competitions at the festival of the City Dionysia. After 507, a man voted in the assembly and council and stood eligible for the magistracies at Athens by virtue of his membership in a deme. Every candidate submitted to an examination: "Who is your father, and what deme is he from? Who is your father's father? Who is your mother, your mother's father, and what is his deme?" (Aristotle, *Constitution of the Athenians* 55). Since they kept the deme of their birth for life wherever they lived, Cleisthenes' demesmen, scattered across Attica from the beginning, became more and more differentiated in interests and loyalties.

Cleisthenes based citizenship and the exercise of its rights upon territoriality, that is, upon a bond with other citizens by place of birth rather than by family and ancestral relationships. To emphasize the connection between citizenship and the land, he named half of the tribes after figures of Athenian mythology said to be born from the earth. What Cleisthenes intended to accomplish by instituting his system continues to be debated by scholars. As it happened, he prepared the way for the democratic reforms of the fifth century by weakening the hold that a few noble houses had over the people through kinship, and opening opportunities for other families to court the people [Frost, pp. 68–69].

Since before the founding of Athens, blood ties through the father line had unified the people under four tribes. These tribes, part of Athenians' Ionian heritage, were named after the sons of Ion, son of Apollo or of the mortal Xuthus and Creusa, daughter of the autochthonous king of Athens, Erechtheus. According to A. Andrewes' widely accepted view [1961], sometime during the Greek Dark Age, a period characterized by the absence of central authority, men grouped themselves around "a local great family" in a phratry (brotherhood). The great, or *hoi kaloi kagathoi* (the beautiful and brave), gained respect from their ancestral holdings of land; from serving as family elders and priests and leaders of the phratry, tribes, and, later, the demes; and from planning strategy and leading the tribes into battle. They forged connections with their humble adherents, *phrateres* (brothers),* providing them with protection and economic help in return for their labor and armed support. Fictitious kinship thus became hereditary bonds which the worship of a common ancestor reinforced. Moreover, families tended to remain in the district their ancestors had settled and to maintain it as the center of their phratry, so that territorial proximity further strengthened the ties secured by kinship. Consequently, phratries were more exclusive, more tightly knit groups than demes.

*So strong and prevalent was this use of *phratēr* that the word, cognate with others (Latin *frater* and Sanskrit *bhratar*) for uterine brother, was emptied of the latter meaning completely. *Adelphos* replaced *phratēr* to designate uterine brother.

By the Classical period, the phratry had surrendered the review of citizen status to the deme, and, in turn, the law court and council at Athens subjected the demesmen's judgment to appeal. Still, men continued to act as citizens through membership in both organizations, and, upon entering the citizen body, foreigners joined a phratry as well as a deme. Although Cleisthenes rendered the Ionian tribes politically and militarily insignificant, he left the phratries alone. Most Athenians continued as always to relate to the *polis* through the social and religious activities of the phratry. "[V]ery few citizens of archaic Athens could conceive of an abstract concept of the state outside of the phratries. For them, the collective authority of the phratry *was* the state" [Frost, p. 67]. The phratry kept its influence because it enrolled sons and, apparently, daughters at birth, examined and admitted sons at puberty, and recognized marriages by celebrating the feast of the *gamēlia*. After Pericles' law of 451 restricted citizenship henceforth to those born of Athenian parents, the ability to prove the identity of one's mother by phratry records and the witnesses obtained through its ceremonies became crucial on many occasions.

In a suit over inheritance, Thrasyllos dwells upon the *phrateres'* formality and careful scrutiny of his admission. His stepfather Apollodoros brought him before his brothers for adoption. Thrasyllos' account of what happened provides a glimpse into a scene often enacted in phratries:

> When the festival of the Thargelia came, Apollodoros led me to the altars and to the members of the families and phratry. They have a custom that, when a man introduces his natural son or an adopted one, he pledges by sacrificial victims that he is introducing a son, whether natural or adopted, born properly of a citizen. After the introducer swears the oath, the others must nonetheless vote and, if they vote approval, then and not before, they enroll him.

This being the custom and the *phrateres* and family members believing Apollodoros and knowing that I was his sister's son, they all voted and enrolled me in the official register (Isaeus, *Concerning Apollodoros' Estate* 15–17).

The candidate's *kyrios*, usually his father, swore over a sacrificial victim that the child was his son. After 451, he also confirmed by religious scruples that the child was born of an Athenian woman. The brothers discussed the case, if necessary, and took a vote. Thrasyllos seems to have been duly enrolled, but, unfortunately for him, his stepfather died without completing the adoption, opening Apollodoros' estate to a counterclaim by his first cousin.

Apollodoros came to his *phrateres* during the first days of Thargelion (May), perhaps because of his declining health. Children were normally registered at birth and at puberty on Koureotis (Day of Youths), the third day of the Apaturia, a festival of the phratries held in Pyanepsion (October) [Parke, pp. 88–91]. Dorpia (Supper Eve) and Anarrhysis (Drawing Back [of a victim's neck in sacrifice]), the names given the first days, indicate that much feasting and celebration accompanied the formalities of registration. The festival was as much social as religious, occasions not rigorously separated by Greeks in any case. But entrance into a phratry or deme and continued membership were far from automatic. Rejection or deletion of one's name carried severe penalties and disabilities: loss of paternity and citizens' rights, including the right to inherit; reduction to the status of bastard and foreigner; poverty; and even being sold into slavery.

To address citizens and join in public life, one had not only to be a man but a man capable of demonstrating his citizenship—that he was the son of an Athenian—by membership in a deme and a phratry. The deme was founded on the principle of residency in a certain place but minimized the influence of place by including members from very different localities. Kinship carried little binding force at the tribal level, whereas the opposite held true for the phratry. However artificial the kinship was in origin, its expression as brothers of a common father solidified the group. The family estate, household cults, and graves of the dead, ties which men shared as *phrateres* and demesmen, promoted the unity of the phratry. Blood, real or fictitious, was a stronger and more compelling bond than geographical contiguity, particularly when the latter was further attenuated by the deme's heterogeneity.

Athenians lived according to two contradictory definitions of what constituted a citizen: birth in a particular place in the land (deme) and blood kinship through descent from a common parent (phratry). Similarly, they told contradictory stories about their origins: they sprang from the earth itself without parents, and they descended from Ion, eponymous founder of all Ionian Greeks. These myths cannot be resolved, since they do not refer to historical beginnings but reflect and comment upon the social and political institutions that define a person as an Athenian man or woman.

In the earliest form of autochthony, Athenians considered themselves descended from kings born of the earth, Cecrops, Cranaos, Amphictyon, Erichthonios, and Erechtheus, "whom Athena, daughter of Zeus, nursed and the grain-giving land birthed" (*Iliad* 2.547–48). "Sons of Erechtheus of the earth," Sophocles calls them in *Ajax* (202). About 423, when Athenians began constructing the temple of Erechtheus, whom they worshipped as a demigod, Euripides introduced to tragedy the belief that all Athenians were autochthonous in their own right. In the following fragment from his *Erechtheus*, the king's wife, Praxithea, explains the worthiness of her people:

I will give up this daughter of mine to kill. I reckon that, above all, the city could take none better than her. Our people did not immigrate from some other place; we are born of our earth. Other cities, founded on the whim of the dice, are imported from other cities. Whoever inhabits a city derived from another, like a joint fitted poorly in wood, is a citizen in name, not in fact (fr. 50).

The following year at the Dionysiac festival of the Lenaea, the comic poet Aristophanes (died c. 385) had his chorus of wasps declare: "Attic men alone are justly indigenous and autochthonous" (*Wasps* 1076). But the transition from the idea of being autochthonous by descent to autochthonous by nature, that is, that Athenians themselves sprang from their soil, did not originate on Dionysus' stage. Orators chosen by the *polis* to eulogize its citizens slain in warfare throughout the Mediterranean appropriated birth from the earth for all Athenians. We discuss the myth-making of these funeral orations in the last chapter.

Thirty-five years before Euripides' *Erechtheus*, Aeschylus compared Athenians to plants in his *Eumenides*. Athena, patron goddess of Athenians, is speaking; her choice of words indicates that her love is that of a parent for her children: "Like a gardener tending his plants, I love this race of just men free of grief" (911–12). The simile prompts a metaphor to awaken the mystery of autochthony. The Athenians *are* plants, and plants, which exist as living things, "prove" Athenians' religious belief in their own generation from the earth. Aeschylus calls them "just men," perhaps denoting the jurors' faithfulness to their oath, but, in this context, we may also read a reference to the metaphysical justice of birth from the earth. Athenians, unlike other men who are born from women, come from their soil and are taken care of by their virgin goddess. Aeschylus gives poetic expression to his nation's founding myth of autochthony, the birth of King Erichthonios:

> Some say that Erichthonios is the son of Hephaestus and Atthis, daughter of Cranaos, but others that he is the son

of Hephaestus and Athena. Athena came to Hephaestus about the provisioning of weapons. Abandoned by Aphrodite, he fell into a sudden passion for Athena whom he began to pursue. She fled. When, after utmost effort, for he was lame, he drew near her, he tried to have intercourse with her. But being a chaste virgin, she did not let him, and he ejaculated on her leg. Defiled, she wiped the semen off with wool and threw it on the ground. She fled, and the seed fell into the ground, and Erichthonios was born. Athena reared him in secret from the other gods, wishing to make him immortal. She put him in a chest and gave it in trust to Cecrops' daughter Pandrosos, forbidding her to open the chest. Pandrosos' sisters meddlesomely opened it and saw the serpent entwined around the babe. Some say they were killed by the serpent; others, that maddened by Athena, they threw themselves from the Acropolis. Reared in her precinct by Athena herself, Erichthonios drove Amphictyon out and became king. He set up the wooden statue of Athena in the Acropolis and instituted the festival of the Panathenaia. He married the Naead nymph Praxithea and had a son, Pandion (Apollodorus, *Library* 3.14.6).

As has long been recognized, mythmakers told the story from allusions they saw in Erichthonios' name to wool (*erion*), strife (*eris*), and earth (*chthon*). The myth itself mediates between birth from the earth, the mystery of Athenians' origins, and birth from two parents, their reality. Erichthonios is born from the earth when Hephaestus' semen seeps into her crevices. Yet he does not spring spontaneously from the earth as do other autochthons. He is sown by a sort of heterosexual act resembling normal intercourse but not identical with it. If it were identical, Erichthonios would be an ordinary god such as Hermes, son of the gods Zeus and Maia; full birth from the earth would render him no different from Cecrops and the others. Thus, John Peradotto observes,

Erichthonios not only resolves the old autochthony contradiction by being at one and the same time autochthonous *and* product of a bisexual transaction, he also permits his Athenian heirs to claim that they are offspring of the Earth, of Hephaestus, whose cult was so strong among them, and even of Athena, and this without any damage to her virginity [p. 94].

Through Erichthonios, Athenians become offspring of their virgin goddess Athena, gaining her as their nurse. The myth may seem nonsense, but by mediating birth from one and from two, it obfuscates the difference between faith and reality and preserves the former from being denied by the latter.

Ancient mythographers organized these myths into genealogies, fashioning an early history for Athenians and joining the present with the time of their first beginnings. In this case, the form does not fit the material, since autochthons, born anew each time, have no ancestry. The following is a selection of myths from Apollodorus' *Library* about kings of Athens, most of whom are autochthonous:

Cecrops, born of the earth, had a body of two natures, that of a man and a serpent. He was the first king of Attica. . . . Cecrops married Agraulos, daughter of Actaios, and had Erysichthon, who left this life childless, and the daughters Agraulos, Herse, and Pandrosos (3.14.1–2).

When Cecrops died, Cranaos, born of the earth, became king and ruled, it is said, during the age of Deucalion's flood. He married Pedias of Lacedaemon, daughter of Mynes, and begat [the daughters] Cranae, Cranaichme, and Atthis (3.14.5).

Amphictyon drove Cranaos out and became king. Some authorities say that he was the son of Deucalion; others, that he was born of the earth. After he ruled twelve years, Erichthonios drove him out (3.14.6).

When Erichthonios died and was buried in the same precinct of Athena, Pandion became king. . . . Pandion married Zeuxippe, his mother's sister, and begat the daughters Procne and Philomeda and twin sons, Erechtheus and Butes (3.14.7–8).

When Pandion died, his sons divided their inheritance. Erechtheus received the kingdom, and Butes, the priesthood of Athena and Poseidon Erechtheus. Erechtheus married Praxithea and had sons, Cecrops, Pandorus, and Metion, and daughters, Creusa, Chthonia, and Oreithyia (3.15.1).

After Poseidon destroyed Erechtheus and his house, the eldest of Erechtheus' sons, Cecrops, became king. He married Metiadusa, daughter of Eupalamos, and sired Pandion. The latter, king after Cecrops, was driven out by the sons of Metion through a civil uprising. He went to Pylas at Megara where he married Pylas' daughter, Pylia (3.15.5).

Sons were born to Pandion while he was at Megara, Aegis, Pallas, Nisos, and Lykos. . . . After Pandion's death, his sons marched on Athens and drove out the sons of Metion and divided the rule four ways. Aegis gained all the power. Aegis first married Meta, daughter of Hoples, and then Chalciope, daughter of Rhexenor. When he failed to have a son, fearing his brothers, he went to Pythia and inquired about the birth of sons (3.15.5–6).

These myths do not relate a history of unique events but repeat a single theme: the failure of autochthons to perpetuate themselves. They sire daughters who are unable to provide their fathers with heirs in patrilineal Athens, and sons who die childless or fight among themselves. Constant political discord prevents the formation of a stable rule, while the dearth of sons slows the growth of the population. The historian of Athens Philochoros (fourth to third century) responded to this difficulty by reporting that Cecrops, "wishing to increase the stock of the Athenians, ordered them to get stones and bring them into the middle, from which he saw twenty thousand of them come into being" (fr. 95). Autochthony insures the homogeneity of the Athenian stock, but its very exclusivity imperils its existence by its unfruitfulness and political turmoil. To surmount the negative aspects of this myth of origins, the Athenians told another, that of descent from Ion, whose strategies blatantly contradict those of autochthony.

Of the three major divisions of Greeks, Aeolians, Dorians, and Ionians, Athenians belonged to the latter group. As early as the sixth century, Solon declared Attica "the oldest land of the Ionians" (fr. 4). It is not certain what he meant; perhaps he believed that Ionians first lived in Attica and spread westward to the Cyclades Islands and Asia Minor. If so, Solon accepts Athenian traditions that Ionians gathered in Attica after being driven from their own country and later sailed westward as colonists of the Athenians. According to the genealogist and historian of myths Pherecydes (early fifth century), Androclos, son of Codros, King of Athens, led the colonization and founded the Ionian city of Ephesus where the royal seat of the Ionians was later established (Strabo, *Geography* 14.1.3). Although modern historians speculate that the Greeks' arrival in the Cyclades and on the western coast of Asia Minor was very different,* several factors contributed to the ancients' belief in Athens as their mother city. Both Ionians and Athenians were organized into a system of phratries and four tribes named after a son of Ion. They celebrated the Apaturia and had the same names for certain months of the year; southern Ionians spoke a Greek close to that of Attic.

*During the post-Mycenaean Dark Age, Greeks came not as colonists but on their own to Asia Minor and the western islands from all over Greece in successive waves of migration and amalgamated into a unity only after crossing the Aegean [Huxley, pp. 23–35].

As Ionians, Athenians admitted descent from Ion, son of Xuthus the Achaean. When the Asiatic Ionians appealed to the Athenians for leadership against the Persians in 478, they invoked their kinship ties. The ensuing alliance furnished the basis for Athens' empire. Long after allies had been reduced to tribute-paying subjects, Athenians continued to exploit their common ancestry. Sometime between 453 and 447, for example, they imposed upon the cities colonized from Athens the obligation and privilege of sending a cow and a panoply to the celebration of the Great Panathenaia [Meritt and Wade-Gery, pp. 69–71]. In 425, Athenians extended the obligation beyond Ionian cities to every ally paying tribute. Symbolic respectively of logistic and military aid, the cow and weapons permitted the representatives of cities to march in the most splendid and elaborate of Athens' processionals and manifested their unity with the mother city. And for this festival, meat was plentiful. In Aristophanes' *Clouds* (423), Socrates illustrates how plentiful: "Haven't you ever filled up on broth at the Panathenaea and upset your stomach, and a sudden cacophony starts rumbling through it?" (386–87). The armor was probably stored in the Chalkotheke, a long building on the Acropolis built about the middle of the fifth century.

Despite such propaganda, the myth of descent from Ion clashed with that of Athenian autochthony. Ion is a relatively late arrival to Attic mythology; he won no place in its list of kings. Far more problematic are his origins as son of a foreigner and product of heterosexual intercourse. Whatever affinities with its subjects Ionian descent and colonization secured were undermined by the exclusivity of Athenians' autochthonous origins and the effects of Cleisthenes' demes. In *Ion*, Euripides explores the difficulties inherent in his community's origin myths and beliefs and achieves a mediation. His play, of course, does not make the contradictions in determining Athenian citizenship disappear, but for a morning's moment in the theater, the power of words may have made them seem less stark and troublesome.

Ion cannot be dated with certainty, but it may be placed in the decade from 418 to 408. In 413, the Syracusans crushed the Athenian navy sent to subjugate Sicily. Soon after, the Ionian cities of Chios, Erythrae, Clazomenae, and Miletus revolted against the empire. Euripides realized how greatly the Athenians depended upon the monies exacted from their Ionian subjects. His Athena says of the Ionians: "The sons [of Ion's sons] at the appointed time will colonize the island cities of the Cyclades and the coastlands, which will give great strength to my land" (1581–85). Those scholars who feel the play appeals to Ionians' sense of pride in the empire date *Ion* before 413, while those who sense nostalgia for the past place it after 413.

That a play would have nationalistic and patriotic themes is hardly surprising. What may surprise, however, is the plot of the *Ion,* which, to some critics, has seemed more a tragicomedy than a tragedy. H.D.F. Kitto pronounces a common conception of tragedy, which explains that view:

> The whole basis of serious Greek tragedy has been reality. The supernatural could readily be admitted as a dramatic accessory—a probable impossibility—but the essence of the whole thing . . . was that real persons in a real situation act and suffer in a real way [p. 331].

Ion does not fit these expectations. Its characters suffer momentarily and are rewarded with lasting happiness. The play has a happy ending brought about by the recognition of a long lost child, a plot device common in the later comedy of manners. Therefore, in Kitto's estimation, it cannot be a tragedy nor even serious theater but is rather a stage presentation lacking any "tragic theme" [p. 336].

Behind Kitto's remark lurk the prejudices and prescriptions for tragedy pronounced by Aristotle in the *Poetics*. Aristotle favored plays about virtuous, exemplary men like Oedipus or Thyestes. He preferred what he called a "complex plot," one that traced the transition from good to bad fortune as experienced by a man of superior moral disposition. The change comes about because of a mistake of some sort. In Sophocles' *Oedipus the King*, a favorite example of Aristotle's, Oedipus, not knowing who his parents are, slays his father and commits incest with his mother. When he looks to the Theban herdsman to shed light upon the murder of Laius, he discovers that he has married and had children by his mother. For Oedipus, recognition of his ignorance coincides with a reversal in fortune from savior of Thebes to incestuous parricide. Aristotle praised conjunctions of this type because they aroused in the audience, he thought, pity for a man suffering undeserved calamity and fear that the same could happen to them. In the *Poetics*, Aristotle assesses a body of literature and draws from it, in accord with his methodology, an aesthetic of what he viewed as its most beautiful form.

During the penultimate decade of the fifth century, Euripides in *Ion* engaged his city in a communal act within the theater of the City Dionysia. Like Sophocles' *Ajax*, *Ion* verges on an abyss opened by a flaw in the spectators' culture. A critic may favor Sophocles' solution over Euripides', but "the tragic" does not reside in a sad ending. Modern readers have become too complacent with Aristotle's precepts to hear the triumph in Oedipus' sure knowledge: "I know this much: not disease, nothing, will destroy me. I would not have been kept from dying except for some dread, evil purpose. Wherever my fate goes, let it go" (*Oedipus the King* 1455–58). "If tragedy elicits our compassion," Harry Levin writes in *Playboys and Killjoys*, "comedy appeals to our self-interest. The former confronts life's failures with noble fortitude, the latter seeks to circumvent them with shrewd nonchalance" [p. 14].

Comedy plays the order of things as an absurdity to be exploited. The coolness to blithely ignore realities ("War is everywhere; Peace is nowhere; I'll go to Nowhere and live in peace") springs from and profits the individual [Whitman, 21–30]. Tragedy involves its audiences through heroes whose actions have more than personal ramifications. Ajax confronts the Other, alone, without the mediations of culture, and plunges his community into a cascading violence that threatens its existence. Creusa and Ion work out an imbroglio of identities against the backdrop of Apollo's will, which changes the identity of all Athenians. *Ion* veers uncomfortably close to comedy in modern perceptions, because the Other intervenes not to test or reveal the limits of the human condition but to expand them.

An actor enters before a stage building representing a temple. He identifies himself as Hermes and the place as Apollo's shrine at Delphi. The god tells the audience the situation of the play and what is to happen:

> There is a city among the Greeks not without mark named for Pallas of the gold-tipped spear. Beneath the crest of the hill in Athenian land, among its northern crags called by the lords of Attica Long Rocks, Phoebus yoked Erechtheus' daughter Creusa in marriage [or sexual union—the poet's words allow both readings] by force. Without her father's knowledge—for so the god would have it—she carried the babe in her womb. When the time came, Creusa gave birth within the house and brought the babe to the same cave where she had bedded with the god. She put him down inside a round basket, intending for him to die. Yet she kept the custom of her ancestors and earthborn Erichthonios. Zeus's daughter yoked to Erichthonios two serpent

guardians when she gave him to Aglauros' daughters to watch over. From then on, his descendants observe the custom of rearing their children among golden serpents. The young woman attached the ornament she had to the child and left him there to die.

Phoebus came to me with a request: "O brother, go to the autochthonous land of renowned Athenians—you know the goddess' city—get the babe along with his basket and swaddling clothes and bring him to my oracle in Delphi. Place him at the entrance to my house. The rest I'll take care of, for he is my son, as you know." I did this favor for my brother Loxias. I picked up the woven basket and put it by the foundation of this temple. I turned back the woven lid so the boy would be seen.

When the sun took flight with his steeds at dawn, the prophetess was entering the god's shrine and saw the infant. She was shocked that a Delphian maid dared to throw her secret birth pang into the god's house. She eagerly went to remove it beyond the altars. But from pity, she let go her savagery; the god aided in keeping the boy from being thrown from the house. She took him in and nurtured him. She does not know that Phoebus is his father, or the mother he was born from. Nor does the boy know his parents.

The young one played and roamed about among the altars that fed him. When he grew to a man's size, the Delphians appointed him treasurer and trusted steward, and here among the god's shrines, he lives always a holy life.

The youth's mother married Xuthus under the following circumstances. The surge of war broke out between Athens and the Chalcidians of Euboea. Xuthus shared its toils and dangers and received as reward Creusa in marriage. He is not a native but an Achaean born of Aeolus, son of Zeus. He and Creusa have tried for a long time to have children but remain childless. They came to Apollo's oracle out of desire for children. Apollo brings their lot to this juncture; he did not forget, although it seems so. When Xuthus enters the oracle, Apollo will give him his own child and say that he was sired by Xuthus, so that when the boy arrives at his mother's house, he may be made known to her. In this way, the boy will get what is his due, and Loxias' marriage will stay hidden. The god will confer upon him, the founder of Asia, the name Ion to be celebrated throughout Greece.

I will withdraw to the laurel grove over here to learn what will happen about the boy. I see Loxias' offspring coming out to clean the steps in front of the temple with his broom of laurel branches. I, first of the gods, will call him by the name he is going to have, Ion (8–81).

Hermes exits and hides in a grove of trees near the temple. We are to imagine him watching the drama unfold along with the other spectators.

Euripides' audiences become familiar with his penchant for breaking the dramatic illusion. In *Ajax*, Sophocles introduces background in a dialogue between Athena and Odysseus; Aeschylus' watchman in *Agamemnon* maintains realism and stays in character throughout his soliloquy (1–39). The monologue, however, is a theatrical convention; when Hermes speaks to the audience directly, he makes them, as it were, an actor. Everyone in the theater gets involved in the playmaking [Goldhill, pp. 246–47]. Hermes not only provides a history; he foretells how Apollo intends the story to end and, with the tokens of recognition, prepares for the denouement.

Modern critics have focused upon Euripides' views of deity and asked questions about divine providence versus free will [Wolff, 1965; Burnett, 1962, 1970, pp. 10–12]. Extracting Euripides' theology from the traditional opposition of earthborns to Olympians as well as from the resentment expressed by a violated woman is risky business. In *Ion*, the "playwrights," Apollo, Athena, and Hermes, create a script and direct their actors, allowing them to improvise until they threaten the plot. They are putting on a play for the audience just as Aphrodite does in *Hippolytus:* "Today, I will avenge myself on Hippolytus for wrongs against me. I am far along; not much is left for me to do" (21–23); and Dionysus, the patron of tragedy who plays himself and his own devotee in *Bacchae,* one of his own productions [Segal, pp. 215–71]: "I will prove to [Pentheus] and all Thebans that I was born a god" (47–48). Euripides' characters judge Apollo's godhead from their own perspectives. At the same time, Euripides uses the gods to please his audience with a message of unity.

Autochthonous Athenians become descendants of a foreigner through a god's violence. In her mournful aria of the third episode, Creusa describes Apollo's advent:

> You came to me, your hair sparkling with gold, as I was gathering crocus petals to my bosom. Their yellow color glistened in reply to grace my dress in golden light. You took my wrist and led me to the cave with its bed. I cried out, "Mother." God and bedmate, you paid favor to Aphrodite without shame (887–96).

A god catches a maiden apart from her mother. The flowers she is picking express her virginity and its ephemerality. The scene tells its own tale of dominance and helplessness. By forcing Creusa against her will, Apollo undoes marriage, the instrument by which her city controls the sex drives of its members. He feels no shame; gods stand outside the structures of civilization. His act operates simultaneously above and below the human condition. But the human Creusa feels shame; she labors to conceal the fruit of Apollo's Aphrodite from her father and mother (898). She sounds the savagery of his violation. Her word for "taking" by the wrist, a gesture used by Homer for warm greetings, also denotes "implanting" of seed. "Led" refers to the leading off of stolen animals, while the "bed" in the cave is also a "lair." Apollo savages Creusa in a den of beasts; through her he bestows upon all men a son to raise them above the bonds of their condition. The god suspends the definitions, the limits put down on the language as well as the institutions that that language reifies.

Creusa and Ion are about to enter a twilight zone of shifting identities and emotions. They stand on a threshold between their youthful, childhood fantasies about Apollo and the identities the god will assume for himself and confer upon them. They are about to undergo the journey of *The Hero with a Thousand Faces*, to borrow the title of Joseph Campbell's popular study of the hero myth:

> A hero ventures forth from the world of common day into a region of supernatural wonder: fabulous forces are there encountered and a decisive victory is won: the hero comes back from this mysterious adventure with the power to bestow boons on his fellow man [Campbell, p. 30].

The mythic journey falls into three stages—separation, initiation, return—which accord with transition rites that proclaim and effect the passage from one social status to another. Rituals to mark or celebrate birth, naming, puberty, marriage, and death are notably similar the world over. Rites of separation remove initiates from their present condition and time reference. Once separated, the initiates exist in limbo, a state of marginality without social status and outside ordinary time and space. During this period, the hero, the mythic counterpart of the boy or girl in transition, has adventures. The rites of the final stage are intended to reintegrate the initiates into society and time in a new status, one which they will bear as adults [Leach, pp. 77–79]. Marrying and giving birth to an heir integrated the Athenian girl into her adult role of wife and mother. But Creusa, raped by Apollo, married to a foreigner, and deprived of the only child she will ever have, dwells in limbo.

At Delphi, she and Ion are on the same precipice threatening Agave and her son Pentheus. Euripides tells their story in *Bacchae*, a tragedy produced posthumously in 405, in which Pentheus has been given the kingship of Thebes but has not left boyhood and accepted his sexual responsibilities as man and king [Segal, 1982, pp. 158–214]. Although otherwise unrelated, *Ion* and *Bacchae* are a part of the Athenians' cultural strategies to effect passage from childhood to adulthood and allow their youth to enter society as husbands and hoplite warriors.

Young men of eighteen underwent a two-year period of marginality when they were "hidden from view" on guard duty near the harbor at the Piraeus and in forts on the frontier. They "went around the country" as a lightly armed defensive force conceived as anti-hoplites [Vidal-Naquet, 1986, pp. 106–28]. As opposed to the hoplite's armor and stationary style of warfare, ephebes (*eph-* those at; *hēbē-* their prime) fought at night, with nets and dogs, and by trickery and stealth. *Ion, Bacchae,* and the institution of the ephebeia resonate with one another, giving insight into Ion's successful transition from child to man.

Ion appears, a youth of some eighteen years, with several priests in attendance. He carries a laurel branch, arrows, and a bow. He seems a vision of the god himself whose praise he sings and dances. He has spent his boyhood in a "holy life"; he knows only that he is "Apollo's." Physically a man, he remains "pure and away from the bed" (150). Although he is contented, he is prepared to depart: "Thus may I never cease serving Phoebus, or should I, may I do so with good fortune" (152–53). The violence he is reluctant to vent against the birds nevertheless suggests the force men need outside the holy precinct. He will soon resort to the bow to free himself from Xuthus' embrace (524) and to a sword to threaten Creusa (1310).

Passage to adulthood begins with a separation from the

ordinary, familiar world. "The mythological hero, setting forth from his commonday hut or castle, is lured, carried away, or else voluntarily proceeds, to the threshold of adventure" [Campbell, p. 245]. The ephebe leaves his house, realm of mother and women relatives and slaves, and reenacts Telemachus' journey into the night in search of his father Odysseus and his own identity. Euripides' Pentheus repeatedly refuses the lure of Dionysus' rites and fails to make the transition from mother's boy to father's son; his last words to Agave underline that failure: "I am your boy Pentheus, whom you bore in the house of Echion" (1118–19). Separation catches Ion unaware: "Whoever you are, woman, your bearing testifies to your noble birth" (237–38). From Creusa he discovers an Apollo unlike the one he has known all his life. Creusa displays a different attitude toward the sanctuary and toward the cave in the Long Rocks. "Why," he asks, "do you hate what the god loves?" (287).

> Creusa A friend of mine says that she lay with Phoebus.
> Ion A woman has been with Phoebus? Don't say that, stranger.
> Creusa She bore the god a child in secret from her father.
> Ion That's not possible. He is ashamed before human wrongs.
> Creusa She doesn't agree and has suffered wretchedly (338–42).

By the end of this episode, Ion accepts what Creusa claims about the god, as opposed to Pentheus who stubbornly ignores numerous signs of Dionysus' divinity.

A second impetus to adventure comes when Xuthus emerges from Apollo's temple and sees Ion. He addresses him: "O son, be well and prosper. That is a fitting way to begin speaking."

> *Ion* I am well. Be sensible, and we both will prosper.
> *Xuthus* Let me kiss your hand, and embrace you.
> *Ion* Are you in your right mind? Some blow from a
> god has maddened you (517–20).

Ion thinks him insane until Xuthus cites Apollo's oracle as his authority: "I am your father, you are my son" (529–30). Thus begins the second stage of Ion's journey. He must determine who he is by determining who his parents are. Ion subjects Xuthus to the phratry's examination: "Who says so?" "Loxias who reared you as mine," Xuthus replies (531). He questions Xuthus about his mother and the circumstances of his conception. He points out the obstacles to Xuthus' plan to put him on the Athenian throne:

> They say that the renowned Athenians are no imported race but one sprung from their earth. I would intrude with two blemishes: the bastard son of a foreign father (590–92).

Ion realizes how Creusa would justly hate another woman's son ruling over her household and how politically ambitious Athenians would resent his exaltation. He prefers to forego the opportunity and abandon the adventure, but Xuthus brooks no opposition.

"Beyond the threshold . . . the hero journeys through a world of unfamiliar yet strangely intimate forces, some of which severely threaten him (tests), some of which give magical aid (helpers)" [Campbell, p. 246]. Such a helper is Xuthus. Beside himself with happiness over finding his son, he confers upon Ion the identity of the son of the man who fought for Athenians. Xuthus has played his part in Apollo's drama and leaves to prepare the feast and sacrifices omitted at Ion's birth (651–53). He is not a fool but a man besotted with good fortune. He appreciates none of the obstacles that Ion perceives.

"When [the hero] arrives at the nadir of the mythological round, he undergoes a supreme ordeal and gains his reward" [Campbell, p. 246]. That ordeal for both Pentheus and Ion consists in confronting their mothers. Agave's son is attracted to her in an incestuous voyeurism made all the more pitiable by his lack of a masculine model because of his father's absence. Pentheus, unable to face his own sexuality, disguises himself as a Maenad to satisfy his desire and watches the scary business of sex from a safe distance. Male, warrior, and lord disappear beneath woman's dress; rather, his mother's "daughter" that dwells within Pentheus surfaces in Greek polar mythmaking when he denies his masculinity. He perishes as his mother's son, torn to pieces by Agave and the other women maddened by Dionysus. By contrast, Ion proceeds with the levelheaded reason of the adult. It is his thread to guide him through the labyrinth of reeling identities. When he discovers Creusa's attempt to poison him, he organizes followers, informs the community, and sets out to exact a publicly sanctioned punishment. He resigns his "war" against Apollo. Shrinking back from learning who his mother is, he is on the verge of dedicating the basket to the god when he has second thoughts:

> I am waging war against the god's good will, who has preserved my mother's tokens for me. I must take courage and open [the basket] (1385–87).

Though scion of Erichthonios, Ion surrenders to Olympian Apollo and consents to be led by him. Others deposited the foundling at the god's temple, but now, no longer an infant, Ion has the courage to entrust himself consciously and willingly to the god. In effecting the transition to adulthood, direct, sensible action succeeds where the ephebe's trickery fails.

Creusa undergoes her own ordeal of deprivation and

suffering. She is separated from her family by Apollo's rape, having hidden her pregnancy and secretly exposed her baby. Uncertainty over his fate and her own self-doubts drive her into despair. Married to a foreigner, she finds no surcease since she bears no children. She resents Apollo for what he did to her; she tortures herself with misgivings over her baby. This is the woman who comes to Delphi to inquire about her child. When her servants tell her about Xuthus' son, she resigns herself: "I will live in a house bereft of children, deserted, and alone" (790–91). Creusa's old slave, surrogate for her father, understands better the implications of Xuthus' fortune:

> We have been assaulted by a clever scheme and cast from Erechtheus' house. I say this not out of hatred for your husband but loving you more than him. The stranger who came to your city and house, who received your possessions, has secretly enjoyed the fruits of another woman's children (809–15).

At Delphi, she gains her true identity as the consort of Apollo and, more importantly, as the mother of Ion. No longer childless, Creusa now fulfills a role modeled upon the social institution of the *epiklēros* [Taplin, p. 96; Loraux, 1984, pp. 223–29].

The invasion of Erechtheus' house by a foreigner triggers Creusa's violence in defense of its purity. Ion's mastery means not only the end of her father's house; since his is also the king's house, autochthonous Athens would fall under the rule of a foreigner, an invader. Creusa protects her father's household from usurpation with the fabulous poison gained from the Gorgon. Her struggle is not hers alone but reprises the archetypal battle of Giants and Olympians. Her strength forces Apollo to alter his plans and have Athena intervene to establish Ion as his son.

Creusa's journey, longer and more painful than Ion's

for being outside her control, ends in a woman's place in Athenian society: she becomes a mother whose son prolongs the existence of her father's household as well as her husband's. Yet her reaction against male dominance alters the cosmos for all Athenians. A woman, someone excluded from the life of the city, is located "squarely at [the] center" of its foundation myth [Saxenhouse, 1986, p. 267]. Ion rules over patrilineal Athens by virtue of his mother and his mother's kinship with Erechtheus and, after him, Erichthonios. Ion returns to his home—marking the final stage of the journey—and assumes his place as ruler and father of sons.

Euripides creates a powerful ending, introducing the Athenians' patron goddess to validate Ion's autochthonous origins. Athena assures the Athenians of their Ionian identity and opens an avenue of welcome and comradeship to the Ionian allies seated among them. Athena commands:

> Take this boy, go to Cecrops' land, sit him on the royal throne. He is born of Erechtheus' sons and justly rules my land. This land will be renowned throughout Greece. His sons, four from a single root, will put their names upon the earth and the tribes of people who live around my rock (1571–78).

Ion could not come to Athens as son of Xuthus, for he would be the bastard son of a foreigner. Nor could he come as the son of Creusa, since children enjoy citizenship at Athens through the father line. Women are the daughters of citizens, not citizens in their own right. Euripides overcomes the problem through Ion, son of Apollo. Thus he explains why Apollo Patroios is the patron deity of phratries, and how Athenians qua autochthons and Athenians qua Ionians come "from a single root."

Seven

Theseus and the Parthenon as Mythic Propaganda

At 9:40 p.m., 15 February 1898, two explosions demolished the forward part of the destroyer U.S.S. *Maine* while it was riding anchor in Havana harbor. Two hundred and sixty seamen and officers perished. The Cubans were rebelling against Spain, and President William McKinley had dispatched the ship to protect American citizens and investments on the island. An American court of inquiry and a subsequent American investigation in 1911 attributed the explosions to a submarine mine but did not fix responsibility for the destruction. The hull, raised from the harbor for the second inquiry, was then towed out to sea and given burial in water too deep for further examination.

The fate of the *Maine* illustrates how myths readily convey different, even contradictory, messages and why public men in particular find them so effective at galvanizing support for their policies. From its entrance into Havana, the *Maine* was more than a physical object and crew. It represented American naval might and a threat of force to the Spanish in Cuba. The captain revered his ship, "the chosen of the flock" [O'Toole, p. 22]. The same ship on 5 November 1895, when it first stood out to sea from the Brooklyn Navy Yard, connoted other things: progress (from wood and canvas to steel and steam), security, and patriotic pride of accomplishment. Before then, it meant jobs and the satisfaction of workmanship. The metal object had none of these qualities; men endowed it with them.

Once the *Maine* became a helpless hulk on the bottom of the harbor, men began telling other stories about it. Among the most vociferous were William Randolph Hearst, who controlled the *New York Journal* and influenced newspapers across the country, and Acting Secretary of the Navy Theodore Roosevelt. Hearst announced on 17 February 1898 that "Destruction of the Warship *Maine* Was the Work of an Enemy" [O'Toole, p. 127]. In a letter to a friend, Roosevelt expressed the same conviction which he also pursued publicly: "The *Maine* was sunk by an act of dirty treachery on the part of the Spaniards I believe" [p. 126]. "Remember the *Maine*, to hell with Spain" became a national cry for vengeance upon a guilty Spain for its perfidious blow to American honor.

These men and the many who shared their views brought the *Maine* into their verbal discourse, not as a physical object but as a word rife with political intent. Words themselves are signs, an interaction of arbitrary sound with concept. The concept, a certain kind of plant, for example, is associated with a sound—"*dendron*," "*arbor*," "*Baum*," or "*tree*"—to create a sign denoting not only the plant itself but, on occasion, wood for a new house, shade against a hot afternoon, a Christmas tradition, etc. Because words are signs in their own right, Roland Barthes considers myths "*a second-order semiological system*" in which "[t]hat which is a sign (namely the associative total of a concept and an image) in the first system, becomes a mere signifier in the second" [p. 114].

Myths empty the word/sign of its meaning to use it to represent a new concept and create a new sign. As a signifier in myths, the *Maine* is stripped of its former meanings, which nonetheless remain vaguely there, and is ready to be filled with new concepts. The ship becomes a word in action.

Like so many others in all times and cultures, leaders at Athens exploited mythic signifiers. The plots and figures of myths were already available to be filled with new meanings. Among the most notable mythic signifiers was Theseus, who became a sign for the Athenian national character as successive politicians defined it. Not a native Athenian, Theseus came from the districts of Aphidna and Marathon, where he was known for slaying the Minotaur on Crete and for raping Ariadne and Helen.

In 561, Pisistratus, leader of the men-beyond-the-hills, embroiled in conflict with factions from the coastal areas and the plains, tricked the people into giving him a bodyguard. He promptly declared himself tyrant. Five years later, his enemies united to drive him out, but in 555 he was back in power. Expelled again a few months later, he established himself permanently in 546 and ruled until his death by sickness in 527.

Pisistratus was the first to transform Theseus into a panathenian hero by encouraging Athenians to identify his own actions and accomplishments with Theseus' deeds. If such precedents were lacking, myths were invented, most frequently modeled after those of Heracles, so that Theseus was dubbed "this other Heracles" (Plutarch, *Theseus* 29). Something besides a cynical politician's manipulation of propaganda was involved, as the circumstances of Pisistratus' second entrance into Attica suggest. The incident is reported by Herodotus, who finds it an embarrassment for the supposedly intelligent and clever Athenians:

[Pisistratus and his rival Megacles] devised a really silly business for his return, as I find it (since the Greeks are distinguished from older foreign peoples by being cleverer and freer from such ridiculous nonsense), if those men at that time actually pulled off such a scheme among Athenians reputed to be foremost among Greeks in sophistication. There was a woman of the Paeanian district by name Phye who was just shy of six feet tall and good-looking. They dressed her in full armor and, putting her into a chariot and showing her what to do, drove her into town. They sent ahead heralds who announced at Athens: "O Athenians, graciously receive Pisistratus. Athena honors him above all men and escorts him from exile into her own Acropolis." The heralds went about repeating this. Immediately, the rumors spread across the countryside that Athena was escorting Pisistratus home from exile, and those townsmen, convinced that the woman was Athena, offered prayers to a human and welcomed Pisistratus (1.60).

W.R. Connor [1987, pp. 42–47] has shed light on the significance of the scene for the mentality of Athens during the sixth century. Connor argues that Pisistratus is not manipulating the ignorant masses as later historians, including Herodotus, think. Leader and people have joined in a dialogue, communicating through the cultural patterns evoked by the tableau created by Pisistratus and Megacles. Common praise for a woman's beauty compared her to a goddess. "If you are a goddess," Odysseus charms Nausikaa, "one of those who hold broad heaven, I liken you to Artemis, daughter of great Zeus, in look, size, and form" (Odyssey 6.150–52). Greeks often dressed up as divinities on ceremonial occasions or times of special joy. Pisistratus drove the chariot while Phye played the part of his parabatēs, a warrior who jumps in and out of the chariot in full armor. Pisistratus' message, Connor suggests, is that "[Pisistratus] comes back accompanied by Athena, honored and approved by her, but as a human being not a superman or god-to-be. He is her associate and her assistant, but a fully human one" [p. 45]. Athena's return to her temple hints at the goddess' own banishment during her favorite's absence. Myths and rituals, shared by Pisistratus with other Athenians, act here and with

Theseus as a force for social unity, binding the leader and led.

Pisistratus took care that Theseus be shown in the most favorable light. He expunged from recitals of Hesiod in Attica the line "A dreadful passion for Aigle, daughter of Panopeus, tormented [Theseus]" and inserted into Homer's Underworld in *Odyssey 11*, "Theseus and Pirithous, glorious sons of gods" (Plutarch, *Theseus* 20). Pisistratus encouraged poets to develop songs about Theseus. His son Hipparchos entertained Simonides at Athens, perhaps to persuade the master of lyric and elegy to turn his talent to Theseus. At any rate, Simonides did publish a poem about Theseus, of which only his description of Aegeus' sail remains. The *Theseis*, a discursive epic composed of short incidents about Theseus, appeared around 510.

Athenians unanimously attributed to Theseus the unification of the twelve cities of Attica under Athens and the extension of Athenian citizenship to all qualified men living in Attica. In Plutarch's version,

> After the death of Aegeus, conceiving a wondrous deed, Theseus joined those inhabiting Attica into one city. He declared them one people of one city, while before this they were scattered about and hard to summon to the common cause. There was a time when they quarreled and fought wars against one another. He went around village by village and clan by clan and won them over. The commoners and poor people quickly accepted his call; to the powerful he offered a constitution without a king and a democracy in which he would participate only as leader in war and guardian over the laws. He would grant the others total equality. In this way, he persuaded them. Although some feared his power, which was already great, and his boldness, they preferred to go along by being persuaded rather than to be forced. Theseus did away with their individual civic centers, council chambers, and magistracies, forming one center and chamber in common for all where

the town was established. He named it Athens. He
founded the festival of All Athenians (Panathenaea) and
celebrated the festival of the Metoikia (Settlement) on the
sixteenth of Hecatombaion (July), which they still do today.
Then, abrogating the kingship as he agreed, he proceeded
with arranging the government (*Theseus* 24).

Theseus appears to have preceded Pisistratus, who
roamed Attica to settle disputes, woo the nobles, and provide financial support for the poor:

> The majority of the nobles and the common people favored
> him. The former he won over through his friendly relations
> with them, the latter through his help in their private af-
> fairs. He was always fair to both (Aristotle, *Constitution of
> the Athenians* 16).

Pisistratus and his poets found precedents for his policies in those of Theseus. The tyrant disguised radical
innovations—the unification of Attica and coining of
money—as revivals of practices carried on by the founding
father of the *polis* [Connor, 1970, p. 147]. When he wanted
to extend his influence into the Cyclades Islands around
Delos, site of an important temple of Apollo and center
for a religious league of Ionians, he purified Delos by removing graves from the environs of the precinct. The bid
for maritime power and suzerainty over Delos recalls the
deeds of Theseus, who overcame the sea power of Minos
and touched in at Delos on his voyage home, founding
contests and a dance whose steps mimicked the windings
of the labyrinth (Plutarch, *Theseus* 21).

Within Attica, Pisistratus was skilled at unifying the people under his rule through religious cults. He "national-
ized" the cults by assuming control from noble families
(who nevertheless continued to bear the burden and expense of conducting the rituals) and incorporating them

in the city's sacred calendar. During his rule, Dionysus was brought from Eleutherae, Artemis from Brauron, and Demeter from Eleusis, and all were given shrines in Athens. The Panathenaea was aggrandized and Theseus designated its founder. By the end of the sixth century, Theseus had become founder of the Oschophoria (Plutarch, *Theseus* 23). In this ritual, two young boys or striplings dressed as women carried branches with grape clusters, the *oschoi*. They headed a procession from a sanctuary of Dionysus in Athens to the temple of Athena Skiras at Phaleron, the city's harbor on the gulf. The youths' transvestism, a common feature of transition rites, was explained by Theseus' substitution of two young men among the women of Minos' tribute.

A few years afterwards, the Athenian treasury, with its metopes of Theseus among Heracles' companions, and the temple of Apollo Daphnephoros in Eretria had been constructed. Both point to the Alcmaeonidae and their leading member, Cleisthenes, for their inspiration. States erected treasuries at panhellenic shrines to display their wealth and prestige in the Greek world. The Alcmaeonidae had lived at Delphi during their periods of exile for opposing Pisistratus and acquired great influence for their munificence in rebuilding Apollo's temple. From information they supplied, Herodotus states openly that they had bribed Apollo's priestess to urge upon every Spartan the need to drive the tyrant out from Athens (5.63). Theseus' presence among the heroes of Heracles' expedition asserted Athens' place among the important cities of Greece.

Threatened by Cleisthenes' reforms and fearing the loss of privileges, other nobles invited the Lacedaemonians to invade Attica. In 507, a Spartan contingent advanced as far as Eleusis before it broke apart in disputes over its purpose. With the main danger averted, Cleisthenes led the Athenians against the Boeotians, who were invading from the northwest, and against the Chalcidians, who were invading from the northeast. Herodotus tells what happened:

> The Boeotians were coming to the Euripus strait to aid the Chalcidians. The Athenians, seeing these reinforcements, decided to attack the Boeotians before the Chalcidians. They engaged them and won decisively, killing very many and taking seven hundred captive. On the same day, they crossed over into Euboea and engaged the Chalcidians. Defeating them, they left behind four thousand citizen-settlers in the territory belonging to the noble horsemen (5.77).

In honor of their victory the Athenians and Eretrians built a temple to Apollo whose west pediment showed Theseus' rape of the Amazon. The force behind the pediment had to be Alcmaeonid, while its sculptures sexualized the victory over the Boeotians and Chalcidians into the domination of men over women.

The myth was another of Theseus' adventures modeled after an exploit of Heracles. For his ninth labor, Heracles was commanded to bring back the war belt of the Amazon queen Hippolyte. Heracles went to Themiskyra, city of the Amazons on the southern shore of the Black Sea. Hippolyte was willing to comply with his request, but Hera incited the other Amazons to attack. Heracles slew Hippolyte and removed her girdle. Heracles' hold on the Amazon was too strong for Theseus to have played any other role than a follower on the treasury at Delphi. But closer to home he could lead his own expedition, and since Heracles had killed an Amazon, it was fitting for Theseus to seize one and bring her back to Attica.

The myth, probably in the form it was carved on the temple, was picked up by vase painters at Athens. Myson produced a belly amphora which shows Theseus and Pirithous in full stride to the left [Bothmer, pp. 125 (vase 9); 128–29 and plate LXVIII, 5]. Theseus is carrying the Amazon Antiope, his eyes on her, while she appeals with outstretched arms to unseen pursuers. Pirithous follows, his head averted back on guard. Antiope wears oriental trousers and carries an axe, bow, and quiver. The scene inverts the tradition of the wedding night, when the groom and bride were driven by a friend from the bride's father's house to the groom's.

The Persians destroyed the temple in 490, when they plundered and burned Eretria for having sent ships and men to aid the Ionian revolt eight years before. The Alcmaeonidae suffered an eclipse after Cleisthenes, until their glorious resurgence with Pericles. Rape, practiced by a national hero, however useful it had been in asserting male dominance over women and foreign enemies, had no place in future politicians' intentions for the Amazon invasion.

In 478, Athenians formed an alliance with the cities of the Ionian coast of Asia Minor and the islands in the eastern Mediterranean. Founded to drive out the Persians, liberate the Greeks under their rule, and seize reparations for the suffering and losses incurred during the war, the Delian League (named in modern times for the location of its treasury on the island of Delos) bound its members individually to Athens but not to one another. Although members could contribute ships or money to the league, most preferred to send money, which the Athenians used to build up a navy.

In 476/75, Cimon was vigorously and successfully augmenting the league's policy of aggression against the Persians when he moved to suppress piracy in the northern Aegean. He subdued the island of Skyros, sold its inhabitants into slavery, and settled it with Athenian colonists. According to Plutarch, "Cimon learned that the ancient Theseus, son of Aegeus and exile from Athens, came to

Skyros where he was murdered" (*Cimon* 8). To cloak their imperialism, the Athenians recalled an oracle that enjoined them to "exhume the bones of Theseus and, placing them with honors in the midst, watch over them" (*Theseus* 36). Plutarch records the following "miracle," devised by the Athenians to explain the recovery of the bones that justified their absorption of Skyros:

> Everybody was perplexed over how to find the bones or to recognize their resting place because of the confusion and harassment caused by the [inhabitants]. But Cimon . . . eager to find them, noticed an eagle, as the story goes, striking a mound with his beak and tearing at it with his claws. Realizing what it meant, by some divine chance, he dug up the bones. The grave of a man of magnificent size was found with a bronze spear and sword lying beside him (*Theseus* 36).

Cimon deposited the bones in the sanctuary of Theseus, the same Theseion where Pisistratus had tricked the Athenians in 546 into disarming themselves. A building sheltered the bones; on its walls were paintings by the foremost artists, Polygnotos and Mikon. With Cimon's support of monumental art, mythmakers continued to draw parallels between a politician's career and the deeds of Theseus.

The conquest of Skyros harbingers the imperialism the Athenians pursued, with brief interruptions, until 404, but the events surrounding the return of Theseus' bones harked back to the previous century. A festival of Theseus, conducted by the noble Phytaedae, was introduced into the state calendar for the eighth of Pyanepsion, the day after the Oschophoria. A holy area near the Theseion was designated the Horkomosion, or place of the oath (*horkos*) that terminated the Amazon invasion. Cimon, moreover, followed Pisistratus and the Alcmaeonidae in characterizing his own accomplishments as contemporary versions of Theseus' acts.

Polygnotos' and Mikon's murals depicted Theseus' recovery of Minos' ring from the bottom of the sea; the fighting between Lapiths and Centaurs at Pirithous' wedding feast; a battle against the Amazons; and probably the rescue from Hades, drawing parallels between Cimon and Theseus, who triumphed at sea over Minos and overcame savage (Centaurs) and foreign/Eastern enemies (Amazons). The murals follow the *Theseis* in associating Theseus with Heracles, who fought Centaurs and was received into Olympus by his father Zeus. Theseus plunged into the sea for Minos' ring and was acknowledged by his divine father Poseidon. The artists, it seems, also followed the epic in enlisting the Amazon on Theseus' side and in attributing the deed to his personal heroism.

About 469, Cimon commissioned his kinsman Pisianax to build a porch on the north side of the agora. The structure, completed around 460, became a favorite haunt and a showcase for the paintings that it housed. So well-known were the paintings that the Stoa Pisianacteios was soon nicknamed the Stoa Poikile (Painted). Pausanias appears to identify four paintings, all of them battle scenes (*Description of Greece* 1.15). In one, Athenians and Lacedaemonians are about to engage in an otherwise unknown clash at Oenoë. On the middle wall, Theseus fights against Amazons, and Greeks after the fall of Troy deliberate the fate of Ajax, son of Oileus, for raping Cassandra. For one of the Trojan captives, Laodike, the most beautiful of Priam's daughters, Polygnotos used the features of Cimon's sister Elpinike. The artist was not above flattering his patron or subtly alluding to his mythic model: Laodike had an affair during the war with a son of Theseus and bore him a child. The Amazonomachy reflects a newer telling of the myth. Theseus' Amazon and the rape have disappeared, and all Amazons oppose him [Barron]. In the fourth painting, the Athenians and Persians are fighting at Marathon. Although Marathon was a stunning victory, nothing was made of it at the time, because the man most responsible, Cimon's father Miltiades, fell into disgrace and died soon afterwards. Since then, however, Athenian mythmaking had glorified Marathon as the nation's finest hour and the apex of its golden age. Its presence among the Stoa's archetypal victories over the Amazons and Trojans confirms its stature as a near mythic victory. The painting showed Marathon, eponymous hero of the plain; the heroes of the district, Heracles and Theseus, the latter rising out of the earth; and Athena, tutelary deity of all Athenians, aiding the Athenians. The victory, then, like the porch itself, appears as the gift of Cimon's family, a victory as splendid as those of the Greeks over Troy and Theseus over the Amazons.

The temple, on a hill overlooking the agora from the west, was begun between 449 and 444, but interruptions caused by diverting workers to construct the Parthenon delayed its completion for some twenty years. The temple was erroneously ascribed in modern times to Theseus because of his prominence in its sculptures, but the discovery of remains of metalworkers' shops on the hill's slope confirm the attribution to Hephaestus. The metopes on the temple's east end, the one facing the agora, have the labors of Heracles; those of Theseus run partially down the north and south walls. A frieze within the Hephaestion on its east end depicts, it seems, Theseus' combat with the sons of Pallas, who disputed his right to succeed Aegeus and were slaughtered (Plutarch, *Theseus* 13). The frieze on the west end reproduces another battle against the Centaurs [Wycherley, 68–70].

The conjunction of the two heroes and the themes of the sculptures are familiar, but, as C.H. Morgan first observed, the poses given to Theseus in the friezes strike a new chord [p. 226]. The *polis* took control over the mythmaking in the public sphere. Theseus' pose in the east frieze resembles Aristogeiton, and the one in the west

frieze, Harmodios. Harmodios and Aristogeiton assassi-
nated Hipparchos in a failed plot to kill Pisistratus' son
and successor, Hippias. After 510, they were honored as
tyrannicides, and their statues were erected in the agora.
Although the Persian king Xerxes looted the originals in
480, their replacements probably resembled them and are
known from copies and pictures on coins and vases. By
identifying Theseus with the tyrannicides, the Athenians
cast him as a champion of freedom and benefactor of their
democracy. But Cimon's time of familial munificence and
aggrandizement through mythmaking had passed even
before the completion of his Stoa Pisianacteios.

Athenians may not have remembered Marathon, but
King Xerxes could not forget the humiliation his father
suffered on that plain. The Persians returned to Greece in
480. Xerxes left the city denuded of much of its enclosure
of walls. Without its bulwark, an ancient city lay open to
enemies, helpless and vulnerable. The Lacedaemonians
did not fail to notice the advantages to be gained from the
situation. Thucydides, historian of the Peloponnesian
War, describes how Themistocles (c. 528–462) devised a
plan to rebuild the walls rapidly to defensible height:

> Themistocles bid [the Athenians] to send him as soon as
> possible to Lacedaemon and not to dispatch the other am-
> bassadors immediately but to wait until such time as they
> had raised the wall sufficiently to defend themselves.
> Meanwhile, the whole population, Themistocles said, was
> to build walls, sparing nothing of private or public build-
> ings from which any benefit for the project could be gained.
> They were to demolish everything (1.90). . . .
>   In this way the Athenians fortified their city in a short
> time. Even today the construction evinces the haste in
> which it was carried out. Its foundations are laid down
> from all sorts of stones, not worked at all but placed as the
> bearers brought them. Many pillars from tombs and sculp-
> tured stones were built in (1.93).

Amid the rubble and broken monuments incorporated into the walls during those feverish days were the disjecta membra of a temple being built to Athena on the Acropolis. Damaged drums of its columns are still visible atop its north wall, put there with care to recall to anyone looking up from the agora the Persian outrage. The temple was conceived in the flush of Marathon and gave the Persian king Xerxes the vengeance he craved. For over twenty years, the Athenians left the site in ruins; they had sworn an oath to let it be [Meiggs, pp. 155–56; Fine, pp. 323–28]:

> I will not at all construct anew any of the temples burnt and cast down by the foreigners, but I will leave them to those who follow as a reminder of the foreigners' impiety (Lycurgus, *Against Leocrates* 80–81).

A few years after the Athenians transferred the league's treasury from Delos to Athens (450), they ended its hostilities against the Persians through a treaty with Xerxes' son Artaxerxes. The peace treaty, negotiated by ambassadors under the leadership of Callias, son of Hipponikos, removed the threat of the Persians as well as the raison d'être of the league itself. But neither the Athenians nor Pericles intended to let go their tribute-paying allies; Pericles had plans for the funds accumulated in the treasury. Shortly before, he had proposed that a congress of Greek cities gather at Athens in order to deliberate, among other topics, the rebuilding of the temples. It was a master stroke of propaganda: by attending, the other Greeks would cede to the Athenians hegemony over relations with the gods. Moreover, Athens had suffered the brunt of the Persians' fury and would benefit most from joint financing [Fine, pp. 364–65]. The Lacedaemonians swiftly declined and, although no meeting took place, Pericles may have felt himself authorized to proceed unilaterally with his imperialism in stone. A note to Demosthenes' oration *Against*

Androtion from the commentary by Anonymus Argenti-
nensis, preserved on a papyrus from the second century
A.D., records his proposal:

> Thirty-three years after the Persian War, [the Athenians]
> began to build temples and fashion statuary on the pro-
> posal of Pericles during the magistracy of [Euthynos]. He
> proposed that the Athenians quicken the five thousand
> talents deposited in the treasury that they collected from
> the tribute in accordance with the quotas fixed by Aristides.

Pericles' motion carried in the assembly, and funds from
reserves were allocated for the magnificent public and religious structures that visibly projected the menacing
power of Athens.

Plutarch, in his *Life of Pericles,* vividly describes these
events and the resistance to such an allocation ("as if we
were beautifying a whore, draping the city in precious
stones, statues, and temples costing thousands of tal-
ents"). Pericles contended that the tribute belonged "not
to those who gave it but to those who received it as long
as they provided whatever it was for which they took it."
In one debate, Pericles asked the people in the assembly
if they thought he was spending a lot. When they responded "an awful lot," he shot back, "In that case, let
me spend it, not you, and I will inscribe my name on the
dedications." The people relented, urging him to spend
on. In the end, Pericles triumphed, and the Athenians
ostracized his most vocal opponent, Thucydides, son of
Melesias (*Pericles* 12–14).

Included in Pericles' program was the Parthenon, the
temple of Athena Parthenos, situated on the highest part
of the Acropolis. Begun in 447, it was commissioned and
designed in the aftermath of Pericles' decision. The people
oversaw its construction at every stage and published records of expenses on stone. Unlike the church, mosque, or

synagogue, the Greek temple was not itself a place for worship; it housed the deity's cult statue and provided a background for the rituals performed before its eastern side. Yet the Parthenon never sheltered the ancient wooden cult image of the sitting Athena. It resided on the Acropolis across from the Parthenon in the Erechtheum, center of the worship of Athena Polias (of the *polis*). The Parthenon held Phidias' chryselephantine colossus of Athena, as well as sculptures that proclaimed the glory of Athens and witnessed the national character of its people. Its goddess belonged to the men of Periclean Athens, and in their temple to their tutelary deity they consciously blended religious conviction with patriotism [Herington, pp. 52–67].

The Parthenon itself conveys that message. The quality of its materials testifies to the wealth at the Athenians' disposal; the subtlety of its architectural refinements, to the skill of Athenian architects and craftsmen and others attracted from all over Greece. The combination of the Doric colonnade with its stocky columns and the slim, graceful columns of the Ionic order expresses the same daring characteristic of Athenians. "They are innovators," the Corinthians instruct the Lacedaemonians before the war, "keen at devising plans and executing whatever they have conceived" (Thucydides, 1.70). Inside the temple, space normally dedicated to the god and decorated with mythic scenes, the Athenians included a human scene on a frieze depicting Athena's devout worshipers conducting a procession.

That the gods concern themselves with Athenians seems to be the message of the frieze where it peers through the peristyle high above the entrance. The twelve Olympians are seated, conversing with one another in two groups. Their backs are turned away from the central tableau in which two girls approach a taller woman. Each carries on her head a stool with a cushion of the sort the gods are using. The woman, the priestess of Athena Polias, assists one girl in lowering her burden. Behind her a man and a boy are folding the *peplos*, the dress for the goddess that the procession is bringing to her. The picture represents "Athena and her fellow deities as interested, but invisible, guests at her great festival" [Parke, p. 41]. It also seems to be sending an invitation to the gods: "We have the chairs. Please come." The presence alone of such a structure, it would seem, intimidated as well as awed the spectator by its audacious appropriation of Athena for its people, the men of Athens.

The composition of the Parthenon as well as its mythmaking reify the fundamental structures of the Greek mentality defined in the introduction to this study. According to Aristotle, the *polis*, an organization of mutually dependent men, exists apart from the bestial or the divine. On the Parthenon the mythmakers seek to minimize the distance separating the divine from the human while shutting out from the human the forces of savagery. When either Thales or Socrates gives thanks for not being born a beast, woman, or foreigner, he identifies the same forces threatening civilization that are found around the outer perimeter of the Parthenon: Centaur beasts, Amazon women, and Trojan foreigners.

The overall scheme of the temple is a procession, depicted on a frieze high atop an inner colonnade, encircled by the myths carved in the metopes and pediments above an outer colonnade. On the frieze, men and women with their children and animals are engaged in a human activity, the solemn procession of the quadrennial or Great Panathenaea. The scenes probably do not represent any one instance of the ritual. The fact that there are 192 men (excluding charioteers), the exact number of Athenians killed at Marathon, has led scholars to believe that they commemorate those slain in the battle to drive the Persians from Greece. Accordingly, the gods have assembled to receive the heroic dead into the realm of immortal fame. In any case, Martin Robertson's suggestion that the frieze shows "the ideal image of a recurrent event" gives the scene an atemporalness [p. 56]. The doings of mortals are enclosed, as it were, protected by the goddess of the pediments and by gods and heroes of the metopes. This arrangement assimilates the outer ring to the city's *krēdemna*, its veils,* which mark off civilization and order from the chaos without [DuBois, 1982, p. 64].

"The Acropolis has one entrance; it offers no other, the whole Acropolis is sheer and strong-walled" (Pausanias, *Description of Greece* 1.22). Visitors walk onto the Acropolis through the Propylaea, a gateway whose roof of white Pentelic marble Pausanias much admired. The structure, left unfinished because of the onslaught of the Peloponnesian War, consists of a porch on both sides of a gate. First to come into view is the Parthenon's west side. The pediment holds sculptured figures representing the contest of Athena and Poseidon over who will be the city's protector. Underneath the pediment in the metopes are the relief carvings of the battle against the Amazons for the Acropolis. Going along the north and long side, the visitors see the metopes of the Trojan War. On the opposite side, if they hazard the Acropolis' precipice and the steep angle overhead, they can see the Lapiths and Centaurs fighting. By now, they have arrived at the end of the north side and turn to the east where the entrance is located. In the pediment they see the birth of Athena. On vases, she is shown being born from her father Zeus's head, split open by Hephaestus with an axe. The sculptors of the Parthenon, restricted in space and inspired by another muse, have Athena fully armed and walking away from Zeus

---

*"As goddess of citadel and city, [Athena] manifests herself in an evocative image of the armed maiden, valiant and untouchable: to conquer a city is to loosen its veils" [Burkert, 1985, p. 140].

after her birth. Zeus sits in the middle of the scene, and all the gods and goddesses are present. Below the pediment, the metopes show these gods fighting the giants, monsters born from the earth who want to take over Olympus.

Artists usually were granted much freedom in choosing subjects for the sculptures [Wycherley, p. 115]. Some relevance to the cult might be expected; its absence in the case of the Hephaestion misled scholars into thinking it was a Theseion. Presumably, the *dēmos*, through its commissioners, approved the artists' plans beforehand. That the frieze was carved after its slabs were positioned proves that it was planned as a part of the Parthenon from the first. Quite probably, Pericles' manager and supervisor, Phidias, the artist of Athena's votive statue in the *naos* (inner chamber), coordinated the subjects which blend the traditional—Centauromachy, Trojan War, Giantomachy— and the Attic—contest and Amazonomachy—with the special relationship to Athena claimed by the Athenians.

The reliefs of the west metopes depicted the assault of Amazons upon the Acropolis. The Amazons oppose Greek patriarchal marriage in both their makeup and in their social system. The mythmakers reversed the ideal of the Greek male warrior to imagine a world dominated by female warriors, women who reject the woman's role of married mother of sons and adopt the man's role of warrior [Tyrrell, 1984, pp. 40–63]. Among Amazons, outside is female. Women hunt, wage war, and rule the city, while men stay at home and tend the babies. The historian Diodorus Siculus (first century) describes the Amazons living in Libya:

They say that in the western parts of Libya, on the borders of the known world, was a nation ruled by women, which pursued a way of life not like our own. It was the custom for women to toil in war and to be obligated for enlistment in the army. During this period they remained virgins; after their years of service they approached men for procreation of children. The magistracies and affairs of state were administered by women. The men, like our married women, spent their time in the house tending to the orders of their wives. They had no share in the army or the magistracies nor any say in public affairs from which they might become presumptuous and attack the women. When the babies were born, they handed them over to the men, who fed them with milk and other boiled foods suitable to the ages of the infants (*Library* 3.53.1–3).

According to Strabo (64/3 B.C.–c. A.D. 21), Amazons along the Thermodon River on the Black Sea

> do their several tasks by themselves [i.e., apart from men], the plowing, planting, pasturing of cattle, and, in particular, the raising of horses. The bravest make much of hunting from horseback and of training for war (*Geography* 11.5.1).

Strabo's Amazons practice agriculture, while their Libyan counterparts, according to Diodorus, do not eat grain:

> The women, the mythographers say, lived on an island called Hesperia, from its position toward the setting sun. ... It was of good size and was filled with fruit-bearing trees of every sort, from which the inhabitants took sustenance. It also had a multitude of flocks of goats and sheep whose milk and meat their owners ate. The nation did not use grain at all, because its use had not yet been invented (*Library* 3.53.4).

Agriculture as a category of thought denotes the male and the civilized condition. The men of Hesiod's Golden Age enjoy a paradise characterized in part by freedom from toiling in the fields. They are sustained by the earth itself.

By attributing agriculture to Amazons, Strabo asserts that they are uncivilized. Diodorus says the same by denying them agriculture, for those who do not eat bread are either gods or beasts. The myth reverses reality in order to create two different worlds that convey a single message: humans are men engaged in agriculture.

Strabo's myth of Amazon mating customs consists completely of reversals:

> [Amazons] have two special months when they go up to the neighboring mountain on the border with the Gargarians. The men go up there, following an ancient custom, to offer sacrifices with the women and to mate with them for the sake of begetting children. Unions occur unseen and in the dark between whatever man happens by with whatever woman happens by. Having impregnated them, the Gargarians send away the women. The women keep whatever female children are born, while they take the males to the Gargarians to rear. Each man claims one as his own, believing it to be his son on account of his ignorance (*Geography* 11.5.1).

A roof was essential for the Greek married couple; the Amazons mate outside. Athenian marriages were arranged, witnessed, and publicized; Amazon unions occur by chance, unseen and unknown, and not always between the same partners. The Greeks value boys; Amazons value girls. Through marriage, the Greek man maintained control over his wife's sexuality to ensure that the sons she bore were his; the Amazon controls her own sexuality and places no value upon the identity of father or son. Amazons are warrior mothers, a contradiction that inverts marriage's sexual hierarchy of male strength over female timidity, as well as the sex-gender roles assigned to each that marriage validates. The myth of the Amazons defends from chaos not only marriage but also the world as defined by the ideal, the adult Greek male warrior.

The statuary of the west pediment represents the contest of Athena and Poseidon. According to Apollodorus,

> In Cecrops' time, the gods resolved to take possession of cities where they were going to receive special offerings. Poseidon came to Attica first and, striking the middle of the Acropolis with his trident, revealed a sea which is now called Erechtheis. Afterwards, Athena came; taking Cecrops as her witness, she planted an olive tree still seen today in the Pandrosium. When strife arose between the two over the territory, Zeus separated them and allotted judges . . . the twelve gods [to resolve the matter]. The latter passed judgment, and the land was decreed to be Athena's on Cecrops' testimony that she was the first to plant the olive. Athena called the city Athens after herself. The enraged Poseidon flooded the Thriasian plain and submerged Attica under his waters (*Library* 3.14.1).

Apollodorus' version emphasizes the rivalry between gods for Athens, a rivalry so heated that Zeus and the other Olympians had to intervene. But another version of the myth, as interpreted by the historian Pierre Vidal-Naquet, seems more appropriate for the west wall [1981, pp. 198–99; 1986, pp. 216–17].

During the reign of King Cecrops, an olive tree and a salt spring appear suddenly on the Acropolis. Cecrops inquires of Apollo at Delphi and learns that the olive stands for Athena and the water for Poseidon. Athenians are to choose which god will be the protector of their city.

> After receiving the oracle, Cecrops convened all the citizens of both sexes to take a vote. (It was the custom at that time for women to participate in public deliberations.) The men voted for Poseidon and the women for Athena. And as one more woman was found than man, Athena won. Poseidon was enraged and devastated Attica with surging waves. . . . To placate his wrath, Varro says, the women

were punished in three ways: they no longer could cast a
vote, no newborn child would take the mother's name,
and no one should call the women Athenians (Augustine,
City of God 18.9).

Evidence for the myth is late and derives from a version
told by the Roman scholar Varro (116–27) and preserved
by Augustine (A.D. 354–430). To Vidal-Naquet, the contest
in this form acts as a foundation myth for the refusal of
the *polis* to admit women into full citizenship. The myth
explains the origin of patriarchy by imagining a time
"before" when women took part in state affairs. During
Cecrops' time, women deliberate and vote with men. Con-
fronted with the choice between the gods, the Athenians
divide along sexual lines, and the women prove to have
control, a situation equivalent to matriarchy. Poseidon,
outraged at such effrontery, threatens to blot out the land
beneath his flood waters, but the men appease the god by
agreeing to punish the women. The myth explains why it
is that women do not vote, why children take their names
from their fathers, and why women exist in the *polis* not
in their own right but as daughters of Athenians.

Although badly defaced like the other metopes by Christian and Moslem pieties, those of the north wall probably
held scenes from the sack of Troy. They assert Athens'
claim upon the great war of West against East, Greeks
against foreigners, that the Athenians' minor role in Homer's *Iliad*, the cultural record of the war, belies [Page,
pp. 145–47]. Moreover, spectators surely drew the parallel
between Trojan triumph and the victory over the Persians.

The bards attributed the cause of the war to Paris' se-
duction of Helen, Menelaus' wife (*Iliad* 3.87–94). Homer,
however, does not blame Helen or revile her; he sees her
as the victim of her beauty and its goddess Aphrodite.
Aeschylus in an ode condemning the war itself is less
forgiving:

> She went lightly through the gates, leaving behind for her
> citizens the din of clashing warriors, sudden skirmishes,
> and marshalled seamen. She dared all and brought her
> dowry of destruction to Troy (*Agamemnon* 403–8).

After the lyric poet Stesichorus (sixth century) repeated
the traditional defamation of Helen, he was struck blind,
so the story goes (Plato, *Phaedrus* 243a), and did not regain
his sight until he composed another poem, his *Palinode:*

> That story is not true.
> You did not sail in well-oared ships,
> Nor go to Troy's lofty citadel (fr. 11).

On the other hand, Sappho of Lesbos (born c. 612) sees
Helen as no different from a man:

> Some say a company of horsemen, others an army of
>   footmen, still others say a ship is the most
>   beautiful thing on the black earth. But I say it is
>   that which one loves.
>
> It is very easy to prove. Helen who surpassed by far all
>   in beauty left behind the best husband and
>
> sailed to Troy. She remembered not her daughter nor
>   her parents. Cyprean Aphrodite led her astray (fr.
>   16).

Sappho neither excuses nor condemns Helen; the most
beautiful woman forsook everything for what she held to
be beautiful. Her Helen suggests how differently moderns
might envision the Greeks if their women had a greater
voice in the literature. Sappho understands how Helen
could feel and act because of her own longing to gaze upon
the lovely face of Anaktoria who left her for a husband.
Homer's Helen, on the other hand, symbolizes what men
ever strive to possess in a woman or in anything: "Mean-

while Helen stands helplessly watching the men who are going to do battle for her. She is there still, since nations that brave each other for markets, for raw materials, rich lands, and their treasures, are fighting, first and forever, for Helen" [Bespaloff, p. 104].

Stylistic disparities in the carvings of human faces suggest that some metopes of the south wall were incorporated into the Parthenon from the earlier temple. The sharp angle on the side nearest to the edge of the Acropolis concealed the differences. The scene showed the combats between the Centaurs and the guests at the wedding feast of Pirithous, king of the Lapiths:

> Theseus allied himself with Pirithous when he engaged in war against the Centaurs. During his courtship of Hippodamia, Pirithous was entertaining the Centaurs who were her kin. Unaccustomed to wine, they drank their fill with stint and became drunk. When they tried to rape the bride as she was being led into the room, Pirithous and Theseus, grabbing their weapons, joined in battle and destroyed many of them (Apollodorus, *Library*, *Epitome* 1.21).

Marriage consists of the orderly exchange of a woman by men and the imposition of curbs upon sexual passion. The Centaur myth derives from and defines marriage by imagining unrestrained lust. The inability to consume wine, the fermented juice of the grape, denotes bestiality, reinforcing the Centaurs' place outside the bonds and ties that constitute marriage, that is, civilization. Centaurs are situated outside the human realm from their birth in Ixion's "rape" of Hera. The Boeotian poet Pindar (518–438) related the myth to illustrate a dictum:

> But they say that Ixion,
> spun every way upon a winged wheel, proclaims,
> under command of the gods,

                              his lesson to mankind:
Repay your benefactor honor's kind return!

And he had learned it well—
   life among the gods had been his
     to enjoy, but he could not
      enjoy it long, when he yearned
       in his frenzied thoughts
        even for Hera, the great bliss
     allotted to Zeus' bed.
But Ixion's arrogance thrust him into
infatuation, and soon enough
                      he got what he deserved,
   a unique punishment.
   Two crimes brought his doom upon him.
He was the first to pollute mankind
by shedding kindred blood,
                  not without treachery;

and then, in the great dark inner chambers,
   he reached for Zeus' wife.
     But it is always necessary
     to know one's limits.
       Ixion's clandestine love
     hurled him into disaster.
    It turned upon him too,
  fool, who lay with a cloud,
fondling a sweet illusion:
                 in shape she resembled Hera,
     proudest of Uranos' children;
   but it was Zeus' hand that formed
   and placed her there,
a lovely affliction, to beguile him.
               The four-spoked wheel

was his own doing, destruction brought on himself:
tumbling in immovable fetters, he embraced
the lesson he proclaims to all.
                 But she, alone,
apart from the Graces, bore him a child,
arrogant and solitary,

without honor among men or gods.
Reared by his mother, who called him Kentauros,
he mated
with Magnesian mares on the spurs of Mount Pelion
and sired the monstrous brood, resembling
both parents: the father above, the mother below
(Pindar, *Pythian Odes* 2.24–89; Nisetich, pp. 163–64).

The myth understands marriage—and society itself—
as a system of exchanges between men. Marriage consists of giving and receiving women. Ixion asks Hesi-
oneus for his daughter Dia, promising a dowry. When
he fails to pay it, his father-in-law seizes his cattle. Ixion
then feigns repentance and invites him to a feast of reconciliation. On the road to the feast, he tricks Hesi-
oneus, or pushes him, into a pit filled with glowing
coals where he burns to death (Aeschylus, fr. 89). Zeus
purifies Ixion, the world's first murderer of kin, a service the latter repays by trying to rape Zeus's wife;
thinking he is seducing Hera, he mates with a cloud.
Pindar emphasizes that Nephele (Greek for cloud) and
her offspring Centauros are unique—each one of a kind
and therefore outside the system of interchange. The
myth derives from a perversion of the dynamics of marriage: Ixion gives his father-in-law a dowry of death and
seizes Zeus's "wife." His son is born without the Char-
ites, the deities who embody the grace or charm that
brings men together and induces them to accept gifts,
especially a woman. Centauros is a pariah excluded
from the reciprocity of gifts [Detienne, 1977, pp. 86–89].

In the Amazon's inversion of sexual roles, the Centaur's
unrestrained lust, and the Trojan Paris' treacherous se-
duction of Menelaus' wife Helen, the Athenians portrayed
the assault of savagery upon civilization emblematized by
the inner frieze. In the mythmaking of the Parthenon,
defense of marriage is tantamount to the defense of civilization [DuBois, 1982, pp. 61–64].

Above the entrance on the east end, a fully grown and armed Athena strides to the right, away from her father. Zeus sits upon his throne in the center of the pediment, his scepter in his hand. Between them a winged Nike flies to place a wreath upon Athena's head. Vase painters favored the moment in Athena's birth when she was emerging from her father's head. But a miniature Athena and a necessarily smaller Zeus would not accord with the majesty of the Parthenon [Wycherley, p. 121]. Hephaestus accordingly has already administered the natal blow to Zeus's head and now leaves to the left. Other gods and goddesses fill the outer portions.

Below, in the metopes, Athena fights amid the Olympians against the Gigantes. The latter are monsters born from Gaia after she is impregnated by Ouranos' blood (Hesiod, *Theogony* 184). The sculptors probably carved them in human form. Their serpentine legs in Apollodorus' lively account of the battle are a fourth-century invention in art and are not attested in literature before the second century [Fontenrose, p. 242]:

> Gaia, angered over what happened to the Titans, gave birth to the Gigantes whom she conceived by Ouranos. They were unsurpassed in physical size and unconquerable in might; fearful to look upon, they were covered with thick hair from their head and chin and had the scaly feet of serpents. . . . They hurled rocks into the sky and flaming oaks. Porphyrion and Alkyoneus outstripped them all. Alkyoneus was immortal as long as he fought in his native land. He drove the cattle of the Sun from Erythia. An oracle decreed to the gods that they would not destroy any of the Gigantes without the aid of a mortal. . . . Zeus sent Athena to summon Heracles. Heracles first hit Alkyoneus with an arrow. He fell to the ground where he began to revive. Acting on Athena's advice, Heracles dragged him outside Pallene, and Alkyoneus expired. Porphyrion attacked Heracles and Hera, but Zeus threw passion for Hera into him.

She cried out for help when Porphyrion began tearing off her clothes and trying to violate her. Zeus struck him with a thunderbolt, and Heracles killed him with an arrow. Apollo shot Ephialtes with an arrow in the left eye, and Heracles in the right one. Dionysus slew Eurytos with his thyrsus, Hecate slew Klytios with torches, and Hephaestus killed Mimas with masses of red-hot iron. Enkelados fled, but Athena threw the island of Sicily on him. She flayed Pallas and protected her own body with his hide in the battle. Poseidon chased Polybotes through the sea to Kos where he broke off part of the island and hurled it on top of the giant. Hermes with Hades' dog slew Hippolytos in battle, Artemis killed Gation. The Fates, fighting with clubs of bronze, slew Agrios and Thoas. Zeus destroyed the rest of the Gigantes with his thunderbolt, and as they lay dying, Heracles shot all of them with arrows (*Library* 1.6.1–2).

The Gigantes, wild and fierce, threaten to plunge the cosmos into disorder. The Athenians' tutelary deity realizes the potential of her marvelous birth by joining the Olympians to defend civilization against wanton violence. As with Hesiod's cosmogonic myth, the east wall evinces the desire to inhabit an orderly universe which, if plagued by violence, at least makes sense.

The Parthenon itself bears witness to the resources and power of the Athenian empire, while its mythmaking defines the image Athenians would project of themselves. They enjoy the special protection of Athena, delight of her father Zeus; they inhabit a land that drives the gods to rivalry over its patronage, and they fight to insure the safety of civilization against the forces of barbarity and savagery. The messages admit no ambiguity and, when supported by the avarice of the *dēmos*, the bold recklessness of its leaders, and the might of its navy, they would terrify anyone who perceived, under the mask of the structure's graceful lines, the fatal certainty of the Athenians that *they* were the civilizers of the world.

Once, the Parthenon's silent marbles spoke a language that all Athenians heard: the sounds of their identity as men, citizens, and Athenians. Now, that voice has dimmed to be filled with the words of creators of new signs, of other observers of the Parthenon and of the Hellenic world.

Eight

Funeral Orations in Mythmaking Athens

Whereas Greeks generally believed a proper funeral necessary for a *psychē* (soul) to enter Hades, the dispensation of the body concerned the living. Restrictions throughout Greece on the luxury and extravagance that could be lavished on a funeral testify to how readily even grief was drawn into the nobles' fierce competition for honor. In the 460s, against the background of the aristocrats' funeral rites, the *dēmos* developed a peculiarly Athenian institution, the burial of the city's war dead in a public cemetery. On these occasions, the city itself financed the burial and appropriated the role of family through rituals that consciously distinguished the war dead from those of individual families, and replaced the ancient lament over the deceased warrior with praise of itself. Although extant orations bear the names of notable orators and surely surpassed the ordinary fare, they pale at first sight beside the Parthenon as statements of the democracy's power. But the *epitaphioi logoi* (funeral speeches) are no less political, no less imperialistic, since the city through its speaker directs at an audience words that assimilate mythmaking Athens to Athens of myth.

Thucydides calls the ceremony a *patrios nomos* (ancestral custom), implying that Athenians buried their war dead in the Kerameikos Cemetery from earliest times:

In accord with ancestral custom, the Athenians conducted at public expense the burial of the first men killed in the present war. They set up a tent where they displayed the bones of the departed for two days. Individuals confer upon their own whatever they wish. When it is time to carry the bones out for burial, wagons bring chests of cyprus wood, one for each tribe. The bones are deposited in the tribe's box. One bier is carried out, empty and spread with covers, for the missing, those who could not be found at the taking up of the dead. Whoever wishes of the citizens and foreigners joins in the procession. The women relatives are present, mourning and wailing on the route to the cemetery. The Athenians place the bones in the public tomb which is located in the city's most beautiful suburb. They always bury the dead from the wars there except for those at Marathon. Because they judged their *aretē* exceptional, they buried them on the plain. When they have hidden the bones with earth, a man, selected by the city, who is not devoid of sense and of fitting repute, speaks a suitable eulogy over them. Then they depart (2.34).

Greeks normally interred their fallen on or near the battlefield; Marathon is not the exception Thucydides thought it was [Jacoby, pp. 42–43; 47]. He also seems to have exaggerated the antiquity of the public ritual. No evidence for the practice exists from the sixth century or from the period of the Persian wars. The authority conceded Thucydides predisposes scholars to defend his chronology, but the *epitaphioi* themselves point to an inauguration during the decade 470–460 [Loraux, 1986, pp. 56–73]. Unremitting military activity entombed Athenians outside Attica or even in non-Greek lands, a necessity that violated the sanctity of burial in native soil. Returning the ashes and bones satisfied religious scruples and allowed relatives to perform the customary rites over their kinsmen, for the speakers do not praise outstanding individuals; the bravery of the dead champions the city, not a hero or his noble family. Athens itself succeeds the hero of myth and aristocratic politics, becoming the recipient of praise spoken by its own chosen speaker.

The public ceremony seems to have derived from a relaxation of the restrictions imposed upon private funerals. Laws confined the setting forth of the body to the house or courtyard within the house for a single day. During that time, kinsmen and friends paid their last respects; women lamented the departed. Funeral legislation curbed mourning in public and kept the rites private. Before sunrise on the next day, the family bore the dead on a cart to the grave site outside the city walls. Men led the procession, and women relatives, whose attendance and dress were defined by law, followed. Lament outside the house was prohibited. At the tomb, the body was interred with simple rites, which may have consisted of sowing the earth with fruits in order to assure the dead a quiet rest and to purify the land for the living. Afterwards, the mourners gathered at the house for a feast [Kurtz and Boardman, pp. 143–46, 200–2; Alexiou, pp. 4–23].

The display of the bones lasted two days beneath a tent set up by the city, perhaps in the agora. Here, families mourned their husbands, sons, and brothers with whatever customs they wished. This concession to familial loss and grief of the first two days contrasts with the rituals of the third. On the dawning of this day, no longer are the dead distinguished by their individual identities or the economic and social differences that marked them in life. Now they are "the dead," an expression virtually synonymous with the *polis* and reified by the organization of the remains according to the ten Cleisthenian tribes.

The wagons carrying the chests formed a procession more elaborate than any family could mount. Anyone could join. Thucydides uses the same formula, "whoever wishes," that allowed access to the democracy for citizens with full rights. In this instance, the formula opens the procession to foreigners. Most were probably allies, a status increasingly equated with subordinates. In effect, the Athenians' invitation, the offer to participate in their democracy, ordered the foreigners to mourn their oppressors.

Setting forth from the agora, the procession moves solemnly toward the Dipylon, the city's main gate. It is perhaps escorted by hoplites in full armor [Loraux, 1986, p. 20]. The high-pitched keening of the women fills the air, soon to be superseded by the orator's sonorous words. As in other activities of the *polis*, women are essentially outsiders to this ritual affirmation of male solidarity. When the dead arrive at the public cemetery in "the most beautiful suburb," the mourners seek renewal through a speech that replaces not only the rites of fertility and purification but also the praise and laments sung for heroes by poets.

Whoever was selected to pronounce the eulogy possessed the requisite skills, since rhetorical respectability was a *sine qua non* for a wealthy man to win honor in public life and protect his property and status in the courts. His task was eased by the formulaic quality of the speeches, which an enemy of the democracy did not fail to notice. In Plato's parody of the funeral oration, Menexenus remarks to Socrates:

> You're always poking fun at the orators, Socrates. This time, though, I don't think the man selected will go on at great length. The selection was made on the spur of the moment so perhaps the speaker will have to extemporize.
>
> Really? They all have speeches prepared. Besides, it's not hard to extemporize such stuff. If the Athenians had to speak before Peloponnesians or vice versa, a persuasive and renowned orator would be needed. But when the competition is held among the very people whom he is praising, it does not seem a big deal to speak well (*Menexenus* 235c–d).

Plato positions his Socrates outside the circle of speaker and audience so that he may criticize the democracy. But like the senders and receivers of sacrificial ideology, those who speak and those who hear the *epitaphios* are one and the same, men engaged in transmitting collective messages to themselves [Leach, p. 45].

Beginning in the early 460s, those messages reflect Athenians' increasing isolation from other Greeks. Athenians responded with a state funeral and an oration which projected to strangers, allies, and the Athenians themselves the image that the city sought for itself. The *polis*, not its agents or mythic heroes, proves the hero of its accomplishments past and present. In the face of their imperialism, Athenians tell themselves a story of their difference. "[T]he assertions and illustrations of Athenian uniqueness, superiority, altruism, and of acting alone for the common good constituted a service to transform Athenian aggression into noble self-sacrifice" [Walters, p. 5]. The city council usually turned to speakers no loftier than politically sensible men to deliver orations over the dead. Their *logoi* have passed away with the ephemerality of the spoken word; those that exist bear famous names, Demosthenes, Gorgias, Hypereides, Lysias, Pericles.

Plato set out to expose the fabrications of the funeral oration in the *Menexenus*. Menexenus, coming from the council chamber where the selection of a speaker has just been tabled, asks Socrates what he would have to say if he had to speak.

> For myself, nothing, but yesterday I listened to Aspasia finishing a funeral oration. She heard about the Athenians' picking a speaker and began expounding on what had to be said. Some parts came off the top of her head, and others she thought over before, when, I suppose, she composed Pericles' funeral speech. She glued odds and ends together for his speech (236a–b).

Plato not only attributes Pericles' eloquence to Pericles' Milesian mistress, he has his own *epitaphios* "glued together" by a woman who is also a foreigner. It is delivered to Menexenus by Socrates, a man who defends himself against a capital charge by "things said randomly (*eikēi*) with whatever words happen by" (Plato, *Apology* 17 c) and who hardly belongs among the "wise men who do not speak randomly (*eikēi*) but after much time and preparation" (*Menexenus* 234c). Plato, in fact, denies the democracy's ability to eulogize its dead when he confesses the inadequacy of prose: "The poets have already told of their bravery in songs. If we should attempt to adorn those same accomplishments with the bare words of prose, we would come out second best" (239 c). Only those deeds which have not been treated by poets, the voice of aristocratic traditions, can be safely handled by the speaker.

To reproduce Pericles' oration for the men killed during the first year of the Peloponnesian War, Thucydides must have heard the statesman speak. He kept Pericles' sentiments for his *History* (2.35–46) but rephrased them in his own style [Gomme, 1937, pp. 188–89]. Although the oration seems to express Thucydides' idealization of Athens under Pericles' leadership, it shares commonplaces and themes with other *epitaphioi* and so holds a topical significance.

Typically, the orator begins by praising the law that established a public funeral and eulogy for brave men. "If I thought that it were possible to set forth in speech the bravery of these men lying here," Lysias (c. 459–c. 380) acknowledges, "I would have admonished the organizers for allowing me so little time to prepare" (*Epitaphios* 1). Demosthenes declares adequate praise to be "one of those impossible things" (*Epitaphios* 1). The bravery of the dead in Lysias' view, however, affords the speaker much to say, so that he moves quickly to their early training and the accomplishments of their ancestors.

The speaker omits details. His is a medium of broad strokes and timeless generalizations. Athens, embodied in the dead, is reincarnated in youths now being educated to emulate their fathers: "I believe that everyone knows that we educate children in order for them to become brave men, and that those who have proven to be brave in war, surpassing others in *aretē*, clearly were well-educated in their childhood" (Hypereides, *Epitaphios* 8). The fallen died bravely, prematurely offering their lives for a noble cause, credit for which Hypereides (389–322) concedes to the city: "As I speak about Athenians who, being autochthonous, have high descent not to be surpassed, I think it superfluous to laud individual families" (*Epitaphios* 7).

Born from their earth, Athenians share a common origin:

> The noble birth of these men has been admitted from time immemorial among all men. Not only is it possible for these men as well as each of their ancestors to trace their physical nature back to their fathers, they may also trace that nature to their whole fatherland which they hold in common and from which, it is admitted, they are born. They alone of all mankind inhabited the land from which they sprang and passed it on to their descendants. The following assumption may be made: those who came into their cities from elsewhere and were called citizens are like adopted children. These men are legitimate children born of the seed of their fatherland (Demosthenes, *Epitaphios* 4).

Athenians spring from their native soil. Unlike other Greeks, they did not migrate into Attica or deprive indigenous peoples of their lands by invasion. They are Greece's legitimate children; everyone else is adopted, as in the orator's conceit, "all men" admit. Plato reworks the same opposition through the philosophical theme of *physis* (nature) versus *nomos* (custom, convention, law):

No descendants of Pelops, Cadmos, Aigyptos, Danaos, or many others live with us, foreigners by nature (*physis*) and Greek by custom (*nomos*), but we are genuinely Greek without foreign elements. Consequently, a pure hatred for alien nature (*physis*) is instilled in the city (*Menexenus* 245d).

Physis denotes innate characteristics, *nomos*, attributes acquired or imposed [Kerferd, 111]. Legitimate children are purely Greek, while adopted children are grafted on the family. Athenians are free of the taint of foreign blood, whether the blood of *barbaroi* or other Greeks, and they are unblemished by birth from a woman.

Because they are autochthonous, they are just by birth:

Many motives conspired for our ancestors, united under one resolve, to fight for justice. The beginning of life was just, for, unlike the majority, they did not gather together from everywhere and, expelling others, inhabit this land, but, born of the earth, they possessed it as both mother and fatherland (Lysias, *Epitaphios* 17).

Athenians tried to cast themselves as different from "unjust" aggressors. Unlike the latter, they fight on the side of and for justice; autochthonous and just by nature, they do no wrong. In the metaphysics of autochthony, "just" connotes the ideal of Greek mythmaking—the Greek male, uncontaminated by foreign and female essences—and puts Athenian violence into a culturally acceptable framework.

Autochthony, however bizarre, communicates a combination of ties to the land and political goals found among early Americans. Men who came to the New World in pursuit of freedom possessed by virtue of their presence on that land "the seed of 'proper' nationalism, and the basis for righteous expansion" [Robertson, 1980, p. 74]. Those eager for new fortunes and possibilities hardly paused over the reality that their freedom most often deprived others of freedom. "We enjoy a constitution that does not imitate the laws of our neighbors, but we ourselves are a model for others rather than imitators of them" (Thucydides 2.37). What the Athenians could not accept was that the allies preferred freedom under any constitution "to being enslaved under a democracy or an oligarchy" (Thucydides 8.48). Pericles repeats a commonplace: the access of all Athenian citizens, not the few, to governance through their democracy. By itself his assertion sheds an ennobling aura around the democracy, but Lysias shows how pride in their constitution was a further pretext for aggression:

> They, first and alone at that time, expelled the potentates and established a democracy, believing that the freedom of all is the greatest source of unity; and affecting that all held in common the hopes arising from taking risks, they governed themselves with free spirits. Keeping the custom of honoring the brave and punishing the cowardly, they considered it the act of beasts to be dominated by violence from one another but proper for humans to define justice by law, to persuade by word, and to serve these by deed, with law as their king and reason as their teacher (*Epitaphios* 18–19).

Lysias draws the following oppositions:

Athenians	Others
democracy	oligarchy
freedom	slavery
bravery	cowardice
civilization	bestiality
justice by law	violence
persuasion by word	violence
service by deed	violence
law as king	rebellious subjects
reason as teacher	ignorant students

Men of cities not under democracies, that is, savage beasts and cowards who resort to violence, must be educated by forcing them into a democratic constitution.

The whole city is the school of Greece. Each and every man among us confronts the manifold demands of life with consummate grace and self-sufficiency. That is no boast for the moment but a truth established in fact, as the power of the city itself, gained through our character, attests (Thucydides 2.41).

Many modern readers of Pericles' speech in Thucydides have been thrilled by "Athens, School of Hellas." Lysias expresses it more prosaically: Athenian law and reason guide Athenian might. However, other Greeks at the public ceremonies in the Kerameikos may have heard a different message in these words. Following the capitulation of Mytilene in 428, the *dēmos* determined "to kill all the adult males and sell the women and children into slavery" (Thucydides 3.34). The *dēmos* felt justified by what it knew—Mytileneans, free to contribute ships instead of tribute, did not appreciate the privilege; Lacedaemonians, defying Athenian naval hegemony, actually dared to sail to the eastern Mediterranean in their aid—and had the power to execute its decision. "When people believe that they have absolute knowledge, with no test in reality, this is how they behave," says Jacob Bronowski, referring to the Holocaust and the reduction of human beings to numbers and ashes at Auschwitz [p. 374]. That the *dēmos* relented and sent out another ship at full speed, creating an exciting vignette for Thucydides' *History*, does not mitigate its intention. Nor does it deny or palliate the menace inherent in the "School of Hellas."

Nevertheless, the orator is a teacher as well as the clarion of a war cry. He instructs the living in the message that the city continues to merit such sacrifices through rehearsing a litany of their ancestors' feats: repulsing the Amazons, harboring the sons of Heracles, and recovering the Theban Dead. This paean of services has no place for Theseus or his Amazon. The rape is forgotten, an embarrassment that undermines the Athenians' identity as the selfless defenders of Greece:

> Long ago there were Amazons, daughters of Ares, who lived along the Thermodon River. They alone of the peoples around them were armed with iron, and they were the first to ride horses. With them, because of the inexperience of their enemies, the Amazons slew those who fled and outran those who pursued. For their courage Amazons used to be considered men rather than women for their physical nature. They seemed to surpass men in their spirit instead of falling short of them in appearance. They ruled many lands and enslaved their neighbors. Then, hearing of the great renown of this land, they gathered their most warlike nations and marched against the city. A glorious reputation and high ambitions were their motives. But here they met brave men and came to possess spirits alike to their nature. Gaining a reputation that was the opposite of the one they had, they appeared women because of the dangers rather than from their bodies. For them alone it was impossible to learn from their mistakes and form better plans about the future. Since they did not go home, they could not announce their misfortunes nor the bravery of our ancestors, for they died here and paid the penalty for their folly. They made the memory of the city imperishable because of its bravery and rendered their own country nameless because of their disaster here. Those women who unjustly lusted after another's land justly lost their own (Lysias, *Epitaphios* 4–6)

Mythic events can be invested with whatever meaning the orator chooses. Lysias elaborates through reversals the strategy that generates mythmaking on Amazons. Amazons fight against enemies who have different weapons and who lack horses, vehicles of swift assault and hasty retreat. Behind the Amazon, informing her weaponry, is the Greek hoplite who struggles against enemies with identical weapons, a panoply too heavy for rapid motion in any direction. In lands outside Greece, Amazons reverse the order of things. They surmount the disadvantages of their *physis* to rival men in courage. When they enter Greece, however, the men of Athens violently impose Greek sex-gender roles upon them: "Here they met brave men," men who stripped their inferior nature of its spurious accretions of male courage. But the Athenians teach them a lesson from which they fail to profit. The imperialists from the East, those who would turn the world topsy-turvy no less than Xerxes, lust for another's land unjustly because they are not autochthonous, and die at the hands of just imperialists. At the Acropolis, Athenians assure all men of Greece of their god-given superiority over their women. Righteous violence forces Amazons into Xenophon's patronizing place for women by killing them. Funeral oratory recognizes no other solution for problems.

Herodotus was living in Athens after 447 and may have attended the funerals. At any rate, he was acquainted with the catalogue of past glories and borrowed from it for the Athenians' speech on the fields of Plataea. The Athenians are pleading their case against the Tegeans before the Lacedaemonians for leadership of the left wing of the Greek army:

> It is incumbent upon us to show you the origin of our national heritage by which we claim on past bravery to be first before the Arcadians. The sons of Heracles, whose leader the Tegeans say they killed at the Isthmus, we alone received after they were driven out by all Greeks to whom they came in flight from enslavement under the Mycenaeans. We humbled Eurystheus' pride, defeating in battle those who controlled the Peloponnesus at that time. We campaigned against the Cadmeians of Thebes where we buried the bodies of those Argives who attacked the city with Polyneices and, perishing there, were left unburied (9.27).

Herodotus' debate probably did not occur in the presence of the enemy. The Athenians' hoplite contingent of eight thousand strong and superior archers spoke eloquently enough for the position they desired. Even so, the Tegeans were hardly going to persuade the Lacedaemonians with the myth of how their king Echemos slew Hyllus, Heracles' son, in single combat (Herodotus 9.26). Lacedaemonians traced their lineage back to Hyllus, who was one of the three eponymous heroes of their tribes.

In Lysias' version of the Heracles myth, Athenians welcomed his sons because "they thought it right to fight it out for the weaker on the side of justice than to please the mighty by handing over those whom they had wronged" (*Epitaphios* 12).Athenians run the risk against Eurystheus without any "previous enmity toward Eurystheus or profit lying before them except a good reputation" (14). Thus they surpass even Heracles himself who, for all the brave deeds he accomplished, was never able to exact punishment upon Eurystheus (16). Athenians again act for justice as they define it, "holding it a mark of freedom to do nothing against their will, and of justice, to aid the injured, and of courage, to die fighting, if necessary, on behalf of both values" (14). If the Athenians, as in Thucydides' characterization, "were born to have no rest or allow any to others" (1.70), the orator explains that they only intervene when they see justice ill-served or the humble downtrodden.

In the events identified with the Theban Dead, the Argive king, Adrastos, led an expedition to restore Oedipus' son Polyneices to Thebes. The attempt failed, and the seven leaders of his army, including Polyneices, as well as countless Argives were slain. Aeschylus in *Eleusinians* has Theseus join Adrastos to recover the bodies from the Thebans through persuasion and treaty (Plutarch, *Theseus* 29). According to Pausanias, "Thebans contend that they willingly permitted the dead to be picked up and deny that they entered battle" (*Description of Greece* 1.39). Pindar speaks of "seven fires burnt to the end for the dead," indicating that customary cremation on the battlefield was observed (*Olympian Odes* 6.15). The eulogists tell the story very differently. Athenians succor the gods themselves, who are being treated with impiety by Creon and Thebes. "Besides all the other noble accomplishments, they did not look elsewhere when the usages of the departed were being outraged at the time Creon prohibited interment of the seven against Thebes" (Demosthenes, *Epitaphios* 8). The Thebans' disregard of the unwritten laws concerning burial compel them to violence. Orators suppress compliance with Greek custom or a king's peaceful negotiations, because those solutions do not justify military intervention or support the purposes of funeral oratory to vindicate aggression.

In the *epitaphios*, historical events, like myths, are transformed in praise for the dead. The disaster at Aegospotami in 405, where Athenians lost their fleet and three thousand men, proves a calamity for all Greece. "Unfortunate Greece had become bereft of men like these, while the king of Asia grew fortunate in having other leaders to fight against" (Lysias, *Epitaphios* 60). Marathon in funeral mythmaking belongs exclusively to Athens, but, in fact, in 490, Athenians summoned the Lacedaemonians and fought beside a force of some six hundred Plataeans. Afterwards, at the celebration of the Panathenaea and three other festivals, Athenians heard their herald invoke the blessings of the gods upon the Plataeans. But the image of a solitary, selfless Athens left no room for allies. "They alone endured risks for the sake of all Greece against many thousands of foreigners" (Lysias, *Epitaphios* 20). The defeat of the Persians becomes a service the Athenians performed alone, a benefaction that humbles the Trojan War. "[The dead] could reasonably be considered so much braver than those who campaigned against Troy. Brave men from all Greece besieged one place in Asia for ten years and captured it with difficulty, while these men alone not only repelled a host from a whole continent but also exacted vengeance for wrongs [the foreigners] had done others" (Demosthenes, *Epitaphios* 11).

As long as Athens had an independent foreign policy, funeral orators repeated an ideology that bolstered Athenian morale and thrust Athenian self-images upon reality. In this, they anticipated the insight of modern propaganda: repeat the lie until it drives out the truth. "A eulogy in honor of the dead or an address for the benefit of the living, an educational homily or a war speech?", Nicole Loraux asks [1986, p. 76], and, as her monumental study of the medium shows, the speeches are all of those things. In praising the dead, they teach Athenian truth about the past to be a comfort for citizens and a boast for others, a boast as fully arrogant and menacing as that of a Homeric warrior. During the public funeral, living and dead draw near for the last time, and mythmaker and audience share an understanding of things.

Despite its hyperboles, falsehoods, and blatant narcissism, "the funeral oration was a true *vox populi*" [Walters, p. 2]. Comic poets refrained from directly attacking it, while tragedians competed with it in lauding Athens. When Sophocles' Antigone (*Antigone* c. 441) defies Creon's edict in order to bury Polyneices, she not only performs rites over a brother, she reprises a wondrous deed of the Athenian past. Exposed amid the corpses of those slain before Thebes, Polyneices is more than a brother. He is one of the Theban Dead. Antigone herself is something besides Oedipus' daughter and sister of Polyneices and Eteocles. She represents Athens of funeral oratory, the *sous-entendu* or subtext uniting Sophocles with his authorial audience. In that light, her family stands for the Theban Dead.

The orators again and again portray Athenians as alone (*monos*):

> "They alone endured risks for the sake of all Greece against many thousands of foreigners" (Lysias, *Epitaphios* 20);

> "They alone twice repelled by land and sea the expeditions from all Asia" (Demosthenes, *Epitaphios* 10);

> "We alone did not venture to surrender them" (Plato, *Menexenus* 245c);

> "We were left alone again because of our unwillingness to commit a disgraceful and unholy act" (*Menexenus* 245e).

Plato's shift from "we alone did not venture" to "we were left alone" reveals that he "perceived the hidden meaning of the *monos* boast, that it also signified abandonment, failure, and loss of esteem" [Walters, p. 7]. In the *epitaphios*, abandonment becomes single-minded action: "[the Athenians] did not wait for allies" (Lysias, *Epitaphios* 23); "The freedom of all Greece was preserved by the lives of these men" (Demosthenes, *Epitaphios* 23); and failure and disgrace turns into glorious death: "They thought that they had to live in a manner worthy of their forbears or die nobly" (Demosthenes, *Epitaphios* 31); "Although we could have lived in dishonor, we chose to die nobly before disgracing you or shaming our fathers and forefathers" (*Menexenus* 246d).

In the prologue of *Antigone*, Antigone leads her sister Ismene outside the courtyard gates so that "she alone might hear" the news of Creon's decree (19). When Antigone asks for Ismene's cooperation and aid, and Ismene responds: "What sort of *kindeuma* [risk] do you propose?" (42), she uses a word that, in other linguistic forms, orators use for the risks undergone by Athenians. Ismene tries to dissuade her sister: "Now that we two are left all alone, think how more wretchedly we will die if, in violence of law, we transgress the decree and power of absolute rulers" (58–60). Her plea fails, and Antigone forswears her assistance: "I will bury him. It is noble for me to die doing that" (71–72). When Ismene cautions secrecy, Antigone replies, "Shout it abroad" (86), because she wants not merely to die but to die nobly (96–97). By the fourth episode, she considers herself truly alone. "Look at me, alone and last of the royal family" (941). With no kinsmen (919) and no ally to invoke (923), she is deserted, and about to be sent to a place "deserted of people" (773): "Envelop her with a roofed chamber, as I command, and leave her alone and deserted" (886–87).

The third episode ends on Creon's decision: "I will lead her where the path is deserted of people" (773). The chorus of Theban old men has concluded the third stasimon when they espy Antigone. She calls to them to attend to her plight: "O citizens of my paternal land, look at me" (806). Together, they sing a *kommos*, a lament usually sung over the dead by surviving kin but here by Theban elders and Antigone, who vents her own grief. Creon marks its end sarcastically: "You know, don't you, how, if permitted, one would never stop singing and wailing before dying?" (883–84). Antigone returns to spoken iambics to describe her future reunion with her family in Hades, to state the custom justifying her actions, and to pray for vengeance upon her enemies (891–928). Creon enjoins the guards to haste, and when the elders react—"This word comes nearest to death"[933–34]—he responds, "I do not encourage you to console yourselves (*paramythousthai*) that these arrangements will not be carried out as proposed" (935–36). Sophocles' choice of *paramythousthai* sharply recalls the consolation (*paramythia*) to the living which, intermingled with threnetic elements of grief, followed the praise in the *epitaphios* [Ziolkowski, p. 49]. The third episode "plays" on stage against the background of the *paramythia*: Antigo-

ne will die not only her own death but the death of the
men whose names are enshrined in the Kerameikos.

Antigone laments her present situation—premature
death, loss of marriage, union with Acheron:

> Look at me, O citizens of my paternal land, walking the
> last road, beholding the last light of the sun, and never
> again. But Hades, giver of rest to all, leads me alive to the
> shore of Acheron, without a share of wedding hymns. No
> song at my we'dding has been sung over me. I will wed
> Acheron (806–16).

The young woman who died before marrying and bearing
children was commonly pronounced in epitaphs the bride
of Hades. Antigone's threnody is not an expression of
weakening resolve or regret over her deed but of what the
early death of a woman meant for the culture. Sophocles'
tragic mythmaking redefines funeral mythmaking, which
confirms what the early death of a man meant, so that
other men will be willing to forfeit their lives on behalf of
the city.

On the other hand, the chorus comforts Antigone with
the manner of her death. As citizens of Thebes, the old
men submit to Creon's authority and chastise Antigone
for her disobedience, but they also voice the subtext:

> Renowned and possessing praise (epainos), you depart for
> the recesses of the dead, struck by no wasting diseases nor
> the wages of swords. Of your own free will and alive, you
> alone among mortals will make your way to Hades
> (817–22).

So, too, Demosthenes says of the dead that they are "Free
of sickness of the body and without experience of the anxieties of the spirit that afflict the living" (Epitaphios 33); and

Lysias: "They did not entrust themselves to chance or wait death that comes of its own accord but chose for themselves the finest death" (*Epitaphios* 79).

The elders confer upon Antigone the praise won by the men interred in the Kerameikos: "These men, having done many things, will justly be praised (*epainethēsontai*)" (Demosthenes, *Epitaphios* 15). "They are worthy of praise (*epainos*)" (Thucydides, *Epithaphios* 2.36); and Haemon grants her the honor merited by those men: "She who did not abandon her own brother, fallen in slaughter and unburied, to be mutilated by savage dogs and birds, is she not worthy of a golden meed of honor (*timēs*)?" (696–99). "Their memory is ageless, and their honors (*timai*) envied by all" (Lysias, *Epitaphios* 79); "It is glorious to look upon men possessed of ageless honors" (*timas*) (Demosthenes, *Epitaphios* 36); "It is just and fitting to give the honor (*timēn*) of memory" (Thucydides 2.36).

The old men find Antigone "alone among mortals," but she compares herself to immortal Niobe who boasted that she was more blessed with children than Leto. An enraged Leto incited her children, Apollo and Artemis, to slay Niobe's. "Niobe went to her father Tantalus at Sipylos, and here, praying to Zeus, was transformed into stone from which, night and day, tears flowed" (Apollodorus, *Library* 3.5.6). Antigone recalls the story:

> I heard that the Phrygian guest, daughter of Tantalus, perished most miserably on Mt. Sipylos, she whom the rock growth like tenacious ivy subdued. Rains and snows, as rumor says, never leave her as she wastes away. Under her ever-grieving brows, she wets her highlands. The god lulls me to sleep very much like her (823–33).

The Theban elders in character protest the comparison of human to divine: "[Niobe] is a god, begotten of god, while we are mortals born to die" (834–35). But, like the orator, they console her again with future rewards. "And yet it is magnificent for a dying woman to hear that she shares the lot of the godlike in life and later in death" (836–38).

According to R.C. Jebb, Antigone wants pity now, not recompense in the "hope for posthumous fame" [p. 153]. Bernard M.W. Knox responds in the opposite vein, that Antigone has her sight *sub specie aeternitatis:* "the hero, pitting himself alone against man's city and its demand for submission to time and change, can find consolation only in some kind of immortality, the quality of the gods" [1966, p. 66]. Sophocles leaves the reason for the comparison to the listener's imagination; any reason is sufficient provided the listener associates Antigone and immortality. Sophocles appropriates for her the consolation the funeral orator offers the surviving kin. "[The dead] are mourned as mortals because of their nature; they are celebrated as immortals because of their bravery," intones Lysias (*Epitaphios* 80); Demosthenes asserts that "Anyone would say that they probably sit beside the gods below having the same place as earlier brave men in the Islands of the Blessed" (*Epitaphios* 34); and Hypereides contends: "If any perception does exist in Hades and any care from the *daimon*, as we assume, men who succored the honors of the gods when they were being subverted likely will obtain care and attention from them" (*Epitaphios* 43).

To Antigone, the young woman consigned alive to a rock tomb, the Thebans' comfort cuts to the quick:

> I am mocked. By my paternal gods, why do you insult me before I go, when I am here to see? O city, O wealthy men of the city, streams of Dirke and groves of Thebes rich in chariots, I call upon you. I possess you as my witnesses to what sort of person, unwept by kinsmen, and by what customs I go to a heaped-up enclosure of a fresh grave. O wretched me, I dwell as an alien among the living but not

as a corpse among corpses, dwelling with neither living nor dead (839–52).

The elders criticize Antigone for being *autonomos* (law unto herself) (821) and judge that "your own self-determining temper destroyed you" (875). "You have gone to the limits of daring and, encountering the throne of justice, you have fallen, my child. You pay in full for your father's prize" (853–56). The chorus' censure concurs with the opprobrium Athenians attached to daring in a woman. "I loathe women who have acted daringly," Deianira utters on the verge of her own daring (*Women of Trachis* 583). Moreover, Antigone has contravened Creon's decree. The chorus in character criticizes a woman who has transgressed a man's word because of devotion to her father's "prize," Jocasta, that is, the incest of mother and son.

Heard with the subtext in mind, the chorus's words take on an opposite meaning. Antigone stands also for the men of Athens in whom daring is valued: "They were bold when it counted" (Gorgias, *Epitaphios* fr. 6); "Who could not have admired them for their boldness?" (Lysias, *Epitaphios* 40); "They dared . . . not only to run risks for their own safety but to die for the freedom of enemies" (Lysias, *Epitaphios* 68); "Noble and marvelous the daring accomplished by these men" (Hypereides, *Epitaphios* 40). The justice with which the Thebans censure her must be that which enforces Creon's decree, a justice which leads the *polis* of Thebes into impiety and which in the subtext justifies Athenian intervention. Antigone's daring is not that of a woman but of Athens embodied in a woman. The elders' censure has another meaning, one that sounds the praises of Athenians. Antigone has "gone to the limit of daring, encountering the throne of justice" and has fallen in death to bury the dead. "They fought," Lysias says of the Athenians before Thebes, "and gained victory with justice as their ally" (*Epitaphios* 10).

Antigone defines herself in terms of the family who determined her fate and for whom she now dies:

> You touched upon my most painful concerns—my father's thrice-plowed grief and the whole fate of the renowned Labdicids. O, the mother-ruin of the bed and the ill-fated mother's union with her own son, my father. From that sort was wretched me born. To them, accursed and unwed, I go, a resident alien. O brother, possessed of an unlucky marriage, though dead, still you slew me (857–71).

"There is some piety in being pious," the chorus again in character as Theban elders observes, "but power, for those who care about power, is not wont to be transgressed anywhere. Your own self-determining temper destroyed you" (872–75). Creon's power may have overcome Antigone, but she dies in a feat of national pride, burying the Theban Dead of her family.

"That the city concerns itself with those who perish in war may be seen above all in the *nomos* (custom, law) by which it chooses a speaker at our public funerals" (Demosthenes, *Epitaphios* 2). In her final speech, Antigone reminds the dead that she took care that each received proper burial:

> I nourish hopes of going there [to Acheron], beloved to my father, beloved to you, mother, and beloved to you, my brother [Eteocles]. With my own hand, I washed your corpse and gave the liquid offerings at the tomb. Now, Polyneices, in laying out your body, I win such prizes as these. And yet I honored you in the minds of those who think rightly (897–904).

Then, like the orator, she gives the *nomos* for her actions:

If I were a mother of children, if my husband were lying dead and wasting away, I would not choose this labor in violence of the citizens. By what *nomos* do I say this? With my husband dead, I could find another, and a child from another man if I lost this one. But with my mother and father hiding in Hades' house, there is no brother who would ever be produced. At any rate, I honored you by this *nomos*, and to Creon I seem to have been mistaken and dare terrible things, my brother (905–15).

Antigone's *nomos* violates dramatic consistency when heard from the lips of this young woman who insists that "Hades yearns that these customs [of burial for family] be equal" (519). However, it conforms to the attitude of the third day of the ceremony in the Kerameikos. Pericles comforts the parents of the dead with the hope of new children: "Those who are of the age for producing children should take strength from the hope of other ones" (Thucydides, 2.44). A.W. Gomme finds it "extraordinary" that Pericles would offer this consolation and not that of other living children, particularly since parents of the slain were likely too old to have new children [1956, p. 142]. But Pericles is not talking about marriage between individuals but marriage as the institution by which the city replenishes its warriors. His is a transpersonal view. In its need for warriors, the *polis* regards individuals as replaceable, as the equal honors paid to the empty box suggest. Sheila Murnaghan has appreciated the relevance of Pericles' outlook for Antigone's *nomos:*

Antigone is defining "husband" not as the unchanging identity of a specific individual but as an abstract role that could be played by several different men. In doing so, she is pointing to the way in which marriage, unlike ties of kinship, is not created irrevocably by nature but instituted by society [198].

Murnaghan points out how marriage depends upon the execution of "a series of offices with stable functions held by a succession of different individuals" [199]. By stressing this aspect of marriage, she believes that Antigone places marriage "in the category of those things it is characteristic of her to devalue and reject. For throughout the play she consistently undervalues human institutions" [200].

Antigone does devalue marriage with her *nomos*, but her devaluation sounds the sacrifice Athens' mothers and wives must make for its greatness. In the dramatic context, she sacrifices marriage to her family, but in the subtext heard by Sophocles' authorial audience, that sacrifice is made to the *polis*—an act altogether right and proper in the real world of Athens. Hers is the higher law of the city, the *nomos* that the city exerts over its fallen hoplites and sailors.

In public funerals, the *dēmos* appropriated the role of the family through rituals that consciously distinguished public from private rites. Once Euripides' suppliant women have heard Adrastos' praise of their sons slain before Thebes, they renounce their claim upon them in language reminiscent of Antigone's renouncement of her own body:

> We seven mothers most wretched bore seven youths most glorious among the Argives. Now, without son, without child, I grow old in utmost misery, counted neither among the dead nor the living, with a fate apart from both (*Suppliant Women* 963–70).

"[T]hey recognize at last the rights of the city over the children whom they wanted entirely for themselves" [Loraux, 1986, p. 49]. Antigone would not have opted to die, depriving the city of her fertility, for a husband or a child, because parents are supposed to relinquish them to the city. Hers is not the attitude of a mother but of the Athens which needs men to die for it and which, in turn, honors them with a funeral. The account of the Theban Dead in Lysias' *epitaphios* almost seems an outline for Sophocles' treatment of Creon, not because of any debt to the poet but because both oration and tragedy rehearse the common belief in Athens as defender of gods and piety. Lysias expands upon a cultural discourse that his audience knows from previous *epitaphioi*. Whether at a public funeral or a festival of Dionysus Eleuthereus, Athenians communicated with one another through the myth of the Theban Dead by sharing and renewing their own identity, their *Weltanschauung*, and their solidarity against others.

> When Adrastos and Polyneices marched against Thebes and were defeated in battle, the Cadmeians would not allow the burial of the corpses. The Athenians judged that those men, if they had done something wrong, paid the utmost penalty by dying, that the gods below were not receiving their due, and that as long as the shrines were being desecrated, the gods above were being treated with impiety. Thus, they first sent heralds, requesting that the Cadmeians allow them to take up the corpses, believing it characteristic of brave men to avenge enemies who are living but of those who have no faith in themselves to display courage toward the bodies of the dead. When they could not obtain their request, they marched against the Cadmeians, although no previous quarrel existed with these men, nor were the Athenians pleasing the living Argives. Rather, considering it proper that men killed in war receive the customary rites, they underwent risks for others for the sake of both parties: for the [Cadmeians], that they no longer would outrage the gods by transgressing against the dead; and for [the Argives], that they would not return to their own land having failed to obtain traditional honors nor leave robbed of Greek custom or cheated out of the common hope. ... Urged on by their success, they refrained from lusting for greater retribution from the Cad-

meians. To them, in return for impiety, they showed their bravery, and taking up the corpses of the Argives, prizes for which they had come, they buried them in their own Eleusis (Lysias, *Epitaphios* 7–10).

Violence wipes away the resistance of the impious Thebans. The Athenians of funeral oratory champion justice to perform customary rites with no hope of personal gain. Antigone acts with justice (451) to fulfill "unwritten customs" (454–55) against Creon's impiety (1068–76) without any hope of gain other than her death (461–62). Like the Thebans of the *epitaphios*, Creon rejects peaceful intercession. That it is his son who tries to win him over or his niece who opposes him integrates the ideology within the family and tests the validity of Athens' stance and the valour of the players' actions. Haemon, in the role of Lysias' heralds, gives Creon the opportunity to yield without bloodshed or further transgressions against the dead. His failure to convince his father prompts the intrusion of Tiresias, the emblem of the Athenian army, to whom Creon submits only after a violent exchange: "Alas, it is hard, but I resign my heart's desire to do this; a hopeless battle cannot be waged against necessity" (1105–6).

Critics have often sought the right in Creon's stand and the tragic quality of his death. He has neither. Creon represents the *polis* not of Athens but of the Thebes of the *epitaphios* and the dramatic stage where, Froma I. Zeitlin observes, Thebes is an "anti-Athens," "the negative model of Athens's manifest image of itself with regard to its notions of the proper management of city, society, and self" [1986, p. 102]. A Creon who equates state (736–37) and divinity (282–89) with his assessments of both, who cannot fathom actions done for any motive other than personal profit (310–14), and who confounds the living with the dead as well as piety toward upper and lower gods (1069–

73), imports the "anti-Athens" of the *epitaphios* onto the tragic stage. Thus, in consideration of the *dēmos* of his audience, Sophocles dissociates the people of Thebes from its leader (692–700; 773–76).

Readers of Sophocles' tragedy have, since Hegel, commonly viewed *Antigone* as a clash of partial rights and an examination of conflicting loyalties and have richly mined and refined this perspective for its relevance to contemporary society. As a message in the discourse of funeral oratory, however, *Antigone* admits no ambivalence. Whatever merits Creon's arguments have in themselves, his actions transgress scruples toward the dead. Moreover, Sophocles' authorial audience would not have considered the play as one of antinomies. Sophocles mediates the opposition of family and state by an Antigone who emblematizes the Athenian state while acting for her family. Sophocles moves his audience, free from the pain of lost kinsmen and citizens, to experience the emotions aroused by the orators. The words of myths were never more active for Greeks than when they bonded individuals into a *polis*.

Bibliography

Adkins, Arthur W. H. *Merit and Responsibility: A Study of Greek Values*. Chicago: The University of Chicago Press, 1960.

Alexiou, Margaret. *The Ritual Lament in Greek Tradition*. Cambridge: Cambridge University Press, 1974.

Andrewes, A. "Philochoros on Phratries." *Journal of Hellenic Studies*, 81 (1961), 1–15.

Arthur, Marylin B. "Politics and Pomegranates: An Interpretation of the Homeric Hymn to Demeter." *Arethusa*, 10 (1977), 7–47.

———"Cultural Strategies in Hesiod's *Theogony*: Law, Family, Society." *Arethusa*, 15 (1982), 63–82.

Athanassakis, Apostolos N. (trans.). *Theogony, Works and Days, Shield*, by Hesiod. Baltimore: The Johns Hopkins University Press, 1983.

Barron, John P. "New Light on Old Walls: The Murals of the Theseion." *Journal of Hellenic Studies*, 92 (1972), 20–45.

Barthes, Roland. *Mythologies*. Translated by Annette Lavers. New York: Hill and Wang, 1972.

Benardete, Seth. "Achilles and the *Iliad*." *Hermes*, 91 (1963), 1–16.

Bespaloff, Rachel. "Helen." Translated by Mary McCarthy. In *Homer. A Collection of Critical Essays*, edited by George Steiner and Robert Fagles, 100–104. Englewood Cliffs, N.J.: Prentice-Hall, 1962.

Bothmer, Dietrich von. *Amazons in Greek Art*. Oxford: Oxford University Press, 1957.

Bronowski, Jacob. *The Ascent of Man*. Boston: Little, Brown and Co., 1973.

Burkert, Walter. "Greek Tragedy and Sacrificial Ritual." *Greek, Roman and Byzantine Studies*, 7 (1966), 87–121.

———*Homo Necans: The Anthropology of Ancient Greek Sacrificial Ritual and Myth*. Translated by Peter Bing. Berkeley: University of California Press, 1983.

———*Greek Religion*. Translated by John Raffan. Cambridge, Mass.: Harvard University Press, 1985.

Burnett, Anne Pippin. "Human Resistance and Divine Persuasion in Euripides' *Ion*." *Classical Philology*, 57 (1962), 89–103.

———*Ion by Euripides*. Englewood Cliffs, N.J.: Prentice-Hall, 1970.

Campbell, Joseph. *The Hero with a Thousand Faces*. New York: Meridian Books, 1956.

Chesler, Phyllis. *Women and Madness*. New York: Avon Books, 1972.

Connor, W. R. "Theseus in Classical Athens." In *Quest for Theseus*, edited by Anne G. Ward et al., 143–74. New York: Praeger, 1970.

———"Tribes, Festivals and Processions: Civic Ceremonial and Political Manipulation in Archaic Greece." *Journal of Hellenic Studies*, 107 (1987), 40–50.

Detienne, Marcel. *The Gardens of Adonis: Spices in Greek Mythology*. Translated by Janet Lloyd. Sussex: Harvester Press, 1977.

———*Dionysus Slain*. Translated by Mireille Muellner and Leonard Muellner. Baltimore: The Johns Hopkins University Press, 1979.

———and Jean-Pierre Vernant, *Cunning Intelligence in Greek Culture and Society*. Translated by Janet Lloyd. Atlantic Highlands, N.J.: Humanities Press, 1978.

Donlan, Walter. *The Aristocratic Ideal in Ancient Greece: Attitudes of Superiority from Homer to the End of the Fifth Century B. C.* Lawrence, Kansas: Coronado Press, 1980.

DuBois, Page. "On Horse/Men, Amazons, and Endogamy." *Arethusa*, 12 (1976), 35–49.

———*Centaurs and Amazons: Women and the Pre-History of the Great Chain of Being*. Ann Arbor: The University of Michigan Press, 1982.

Fine, John V. A. *The Ancient Greeks: A Critical History*. Cambridge, Mass.: Harvard University Press, 1983.

Fish, Stanley. *Is There a Text in This Class?: The Authority of Interpretative Communities*. Cambridge, Mass.: Harvard University Press, 1980.

Foley, Helene P. "The Female 'Intruder' Reconsidered: Women in Aristophanes' *Lysistrata* and *Ecclesiazusae*." *Classical Philology*, 77 (1982), 1–21.

Fontenrose, Joseph. *Python: A Study of Delphic Myth and Its Origins*. Berkeley: University of California Press, 1959.

Frost, Frank J. "Tribal Politics and the Civic State." *American Journal of Ancient History*, 1 (1976), 66–75.

Gardner, John and John Maier. *Gilgamesh. Translated from the Sîn-leqi-unninnī Version*. New York: Vintage Books, 1985.

Gargarin, Michael. "The Vote of Athena." *American Journal of Philology*, 96 (1975), 121–27.

Girard, René. "The Plague in Literature and Myth." *Texas Studies in Literature and Language*, 15 (1974), 833–50.

———*Violence and the Sacred*. Translated by Patrick Gregory. Baltimore: The Johns Hopkins University Press, 1977.

Goldhill, Simon. *Reading Greek Tragedy*. Cambridge: Cambridge University Press, 1986.

Gomme, A. W. *Essays in Greek History and Literature*. Oxford: Blackwell, 1937.

———*A Historical Commentary on Thucydides*, vol. 2. Oxford: Oxford University Press, 1956.

Gould, John. "Law, Custom and Myth: Aspects of the Social Position of Women in Classical Athens." *Journal of Hellenic Studies*, 100 (1980), 38–59.

Gouldner, Alvin W. *Enter Plato: Classical Greece and the Origins of Social Theory*. New York: Basic Books, 1965.

Harrison, A. R. W. *The Law of Athens I: The Family and Property*. Oxford: Oxford University Press, 1968.

Havelock, Eric A. *Preface to Plato*. New York: Grosset and Dunlap, 1963.

———*The Literate Revolution in Greece and Its Cultural Consequences*. Princeton: Princeton University Press, 1982.

Herington, C. J. *Athena Parthenos and Athena Polias: A Study in the Religion of Periclean Athens*. Manchester: Manchester University Press, 1955.

Huxley, G. L. *The Early Ionians*. London: Faber & Faber, 1966.

Jacoby, F. *"Patrios Nomos:* State Burial in Athens and the Public Cemetery in the Kerameikos." *Journal of Hellenic Studies* 64 (1944), 37–66.

Jebb, R. C. *Sophocles: The Plays and Fragments. III: The Antigone.* Cambridge: Cambridge University Press, 1888.

Kerferd, G. B. *The Sophistic Movement.* Cambridge: Cambridge University Press, 1981.

Keuls, Eva C. *The Reign of the Phallus: Sexual Politics in Ancient Athens.* New York: Harper and Row, 1985.

Kirk, G. S. *Myth: Its Meanings and Functions in Ancient and Other Cultures.* Berkeley: University of California Press; Cambridge: Cambridge University Press, 1970.

———*The Nature of Greek Myths.* Middlesex: Penguin Books, 1974.

Kitto, H. D. F. *Greek Tragedy: A Literary Study.* Garden City, N.J.: Doubleday, 1954.

Knox, Bernard M. W. "The *Ajax* of Sophocles." *Harvard Studies in Classical Philology,* 65 (1961), 1–37.

———*The Heroic Temper: Studies in Sophoclean Tragedy.* Berkeley: University of California Press, 1966.

Kurtz, Donna C. and John Boardman. *Greek Burial Customs.* Ithaca, N.Y.: Cornell University Press, 1971.

Lacey, W. K. *The Family in Classical Greece.* London: Thames and Hudson, 1968.

Lattimore, Richmond (trans.). *The Iliad of Homer.* Chicago: The University of Chicago Press, 1951.

Leach, Edmund. *Culture and Communication.* Cambridge: Cambridge University Press, 1976.

Levin, Harry. *Playboys and Killjoys: An Essay on the Theory and Practice of Comedy.* New York: Oxford University Press, 1987.

Littleton, C. Scott. "The 'Kingship in Heaven' Theme." In *Myth and Law among the Indo-Europeans,* edited by Jaan Puhvel, 83–121. Berkeley: University of California Press, 1970.

Loraux, Nicole. *Les enfants d'Athéna. Idées athéniennes sur la citoyenneté et la division des sexes.* 2nd ed. Paris: Maspero, 1984.

———*The Invention of Athens. The Funeral Oration in the Classical City.* Translated by Alan Sheridan. Cambridge, Mass.: Harvard University Press, 1986.

Meiggs, Russell. "The Political Implications of the Parthenon."
    Greece & Rome, 10 (1963), 36–45.
———*The Athenian Empire*. Oxford: Oxford University Press,
    1972.
Meritt, B. D. and H. T. Wade-Gery. "The Dating of Documents
    to the Mid-Fifth Century—I." *Journal of Hellenic Studies*,
    82 (1962), 67–74.
Morgan, Ch. H. "The Sculptures of the Hephaisteion." *Hesperia*
    31 (1962) 210–35.
Munich, Adrienne. "Notorious Signs, Feminist Criticism and
    Literary Tradition." In *Making a Difference: Feminist Literary
    Criticism*, edited by Gayle Greene and Coppélia Kahn,
    238–59. London: Methuen, 1985.
Murnaghan, Sheila. "*Antigone* 904–920 and the Institution of
    Marriage." *American Journal of Philology*, 107 (1986), 192–
    207.
Murray, Gilbert. *Aeschylus, The Creator of Tragedy*. Oxford: Oxford
    University Press, 1940.
Nagy, Gregory. *The Best of the Achaeans: Concepts of the Hero in
    Archaic Greek Poetry*. Baltimore: The Johns Hopkins Uni-
    versity Press, 1979.
Nisetich, Frank J. *Pindar's Victory Odes*. Baltimore: The Johns
    Hopkins University Press, 1980.
Ortner, Sherry B. "Is Female to Male as Nature Is to Culture?".
    In *Woman, Culture, and Society*, edited by Michelle Zim-
    balist Rosaldo and Louise Lamphere, 67–87. Stanford:
    Stanford University Press, 1974.
O'Toole, G. J. A. *The Spanish War, an American Epic—1898*. New
    York: W.W. Norton, 1984.
Otto, Walter F. *Dionysus: Myth and Cult*. Translated by Robert
    B. Palmer. Bloomington: Indiana University Press, 1965.
Owen, A. S. *Euripides' Ion*. Oxford: Oxford University Press,
    1939.
Page, Denys L. *History and the Homeric 'Iliad'*. Berkeley: Univer-
    sity of California Press, 1963.
Parke, H. W. *Festivals of the Athenians*. London: Thames and
    Hudson, 1977.
Parry, Milman. *The Making of Homeric Verse: The Collected Papers
    of Milman Parry*, edited by Adam Parry. Oxford: Oxford
    University Press, 1971.

Patterson, Cynthia. *Pericles' Citizenship Law of 451–50 B.C.* New York: Arno Press, 1981.

Pavlovskis, Zoja. "The Voice of the Actor in Greek Tragedy." *The Classical World,* 71 (1977), 113–23.

Peradotto, John. "Oedipus and Erichthonius: Some Observations on Paradigmatic and Syntagmatic Order." *Arethusa,* 10 (1977), 85–101.

Pomeroy, Sarah B. *Goddesses, Whores, Wives, and Slaves. Women in Classical Antiquity.* New York: Schocken, 1975.

Rabinowitz, Peter J. "Shifting Stands, Shifting Standards: Reading, Interpretation, and Literary Judgment." *Arethusa* 19 (1986) 115–34.

Redfield, James M. *Nature and Culture in the 'Iliad': The Tragedy of Hector.* Chicago: The University of Chicago Press, 1975.

Robertson, James Oliver. *American Myth, American Reality.* New York: Hill & Wang, 1980.

Robertson, Martin. "The Sculptures of the Parthenon." *Greece & Rome,* 10 (1963), 46–61.

Rosaldo, Michelle Zimbalist. "Woman, Culture, and Society: A Theoretical Overview." In *Woman, Culture, and Society,* edited by Michelle Zimbalist Rosaldo and Louise Lamphere, 17–42. Stanford: Stanford University Press, 1974.

Rose, H. J. *A Handbook of Greek Literature from Homer to the Age of Lucan.* New York: E.P. Dutton, 1960.

Rudhardt, Jean. *Notions fondamentales de la pensée religieuse et actes constitutifs du culte dans la Grèce classique.* Geneva: Droz, 1958.

Saxenhouse, Arlene W. "Myths and the Origins of Cities: Reflections on the Autochthony Theme in Euripides' *Ion.*" In *Greek Tragedy and Political Theory,* 252–73. Berkeley: University of California Press, 1986.

Schein, Seth L. *The Mortal Hero: An Introduction to Homer's 'Iliad'.* Berkeley: University of California Press, 1984.

Schulz, Charles M. *You've Got To Be You, Snoopy.* Greenwich, Conn.: Fawcett, 1976.

Sealey, Raphael. *The Athenian Republic: Democracy or the Rule of Law?* University Park: The Pennsylvania State University Press, 1987.

Segal, Charles. *Tragedy and Civilization: An Interpretation of Sophocles.* Cambridge, Mass.: Harvard University Press, 1981.

————Dionysiac Poetics and Euripides' 'Bacchae'. Princeton: Princeton University Press, 1982.
Shive, David. *Naming Achilles*. New York: Oxford University Press, 1987.
Snodgrass, A. M. *Arms and Armour of the Greeks*. London: Thames and Hudson, 1967.
Stanford, W. B. *Sophocles. Ajax*. London: Macmillan & Co., 1963.
————*Greek Tragedy and the Emotions: An Introductory Study*. London: Routledge & Kegan Paul, 1983.
Stengel, Paul. *Opferbraüche der Griechen*. Leipzig: Teubner, 1910.
Taplin, Oliver. *Greek Tragedy in Action*. Berkeley: University of California Press, 1978.
Tyrrell, Wm. Blake. *Amazons: A Study in Athenian Mythmaking*. Baltimore: The Johns Hopkins University Press, 1984.
————"The Unity of Sophocles' *Ajax*." *Arethusa*, 18 (1985), 155–85.
Vernant, Jean-Pierre. "Greek Tragedy: Problems of Interpretation." In *The Structuralist Controversy: The Languages of Criticism and the Sciences of Man*, edited by Richard Macksey and Eugenio Donato, 273–95. Baltimore: The Johns Hopkins University Press, 1970.
————"Sacrifice et alimentation humaine à propos du 'Prométhée d'Hésiode'." *Annali della Scuola Normale Superiore di Pisa*, 3 (1977), 905–40.
————*Myth and Society in Ancient Greece*. Translated by Janet Lloyd. Atlantic Highlands, N.J.: Humanities Press, 1980.
————"Théorie générale du sacrifice et mise à mort dans la θυσία grecque." In *Le Sacrifice dans l'antiquité, Entretiens sur l'antiquité classique*, 27 (1981), 1–21.
————*The Origins of Greek Thought*. Translated from the French. Ithaca, N.Y.: Cornell University Press, 1982.
————and Pierre Vidal-Naquet. *Myth and Tragedy in Ancient Greece*. Translated by Janet Lloyd. New York: Zone Books, 1988.
Verrall, A. W. *The 'Eumenides' of Aeschylus*. London: Macmillan & Co., 1908.
Vidal-Naquet, Pierre. "Le chasseur noir et l'origine de l'éphébie athénienne." *Annales: Economies, Sociétés, Civilisations*, 23 (1968), 947–64.
————"Slavery and the Rule of Women in Tradition, Myth

and Utopia." In *Myth, Religion and Society*, edited by R. L. Gordon, 187–200. Cambridge: Cambridge University Press, 1981.

———*The Black Hunter*. Baltimore: The Johns Hopkins University Press, 1986.

Walker, Susan. "Women and Housing in Classical Greece: the Archaeological Evidence." In *Images of Women in Antiquity*, edited by Averil Cameron and Amélie Kuhrt, 81–91. London: Croom Helm, 1983.

Walters, Kenneth R. "Rhetoric as Ritual: The Semiotics of the Attic Funeral Oration." *Florilegium*, 2 (1980), 1–27.

West, M. L. (ed.). *Theogony*, by Hesiod. Oxford: Oxford University Press, 1966.

Whitman, Cedric H. *Aristophanes and the Comic Hero*. Cambridge, Mass.: Harvard University Press, 1964.

Winnington-Ingram, R. P. *Sophocles: An Interpretation*. Cambridge: Cambridge University Press, 1980.

Wolff, Christian. "The Design and Myth in Euripides' *Ion*." *Harvard Studies in Classical Philology*, 69 (1965), 169–94.

Wolff, Hans Julius. "Marriage Law and Family Organization in Ancient Athens." *Traditio*, 2 (1944), 43–95.

Wycherley, R. E. *The Stones of Athens*. Princeton: Princeton University Press, 1978.

Zeitlin, Froma I. "The Dynamics of Misogyny: Myth and Mythmaking in the *Oresteia*." *Arethusa*, 11 (1978), 149–84.

———"Thebes: Theater of Self and Society in Athenian Drama." In *Greek Tragedy and Political Theory*, edited by J. Peter Euben, 101–41. Berkeley: University of California Press, 1986.

Ziolkowski, John E. *Thucydides and the Tradition of Funeral Speeches at Athens*. Salem, N.H.: Ayer Company, 1985.

Index

225